PICKER'S BIBLE

2nd Edition

BIBLE

HOW TO PICK ANTIQUES LIKE THE PROS

by Joe Willard

Published by

Krause Publications, a division of F+W Media, Inc.
700 East State Street • Iola, WI 54990-0001
715-445-2214 • 888-457-2873
www.krausebooks.com

To order books or other products call toll-free 1-800-258-0929
or visit us online at www.krausebooks.com

Cover photo copyright Shutterstock/Multiart.
Back cover photo: Sotheby's.

ISBN-13: 978-1-4402-4035-5
ISBN-10: 1-4402-4035-3

Cover Design by Sharon Bartsch
Designed by Dane Royer
Edited by Kristine Manty
Printed in the United States of America

Acknowledgments

Thanks to the following people for their help:

To my wife, whose expertise and patience were necessary as my assistant to this project. She has been the best partner I could have ever hoped for as we went out to do all of these things.

To Dad, who always encouraged me to be a salesman and show there are no limits to how much you can sell!

To Mom, who, when I was young, was so delighted with all the junk I brought home. She put up with the stuff I took apart to see how it was built.

My picker friends, who teach me, whether they know it or not. They shared tips, stuff, and experiences as truly professional pickers.

Thanks to all of the other collectors, colleagues, dealers, and customers who helped me, sold to me, and bought from me.

For more information, visit www.pickersbible.com.

About the Author

After working more than 30 years in wholesale electronic distribution and retiring as a VP/general manager, Joe Willard has made his living picking antiques and industrial goods for the past 15 years. While he is attracted to "guy stuff"—tools, cameras, radios, anything with grime—he is always on the lookout for treasure in other people's trash.

Contents

························

Professor Tom Perera, Ph.D., an antiques dealer, stands next to an original German World War II Enigma cipher machine at the Brimfield Antiques Show. How much do you think the selling price was? See Page 68 for the answer. Also see Chapter 4 for more about Brimfield.

Clifford Smith with his "trench art" find at Brimfield Antiques Show. Notice the beautiful rose engraved on the artillery shell by a soldier.

Introduction

We have all seen the adventure spy drama movies, where the super spy will enter a room and in a split second, see everything available, and make some sort of bomb or trap for the bad guys because "it's in their training."

I heard a friend once say he read a book with something similar about prehistoric man. How, by instinct and experience, he could, at any point, notice anything and everything in his close environment that could be used as a tool or food, or for survival. It's in you, too. Once you learn what certain things are worth, and find a good venue or sale, you will see these "powers" in you to quickly scan a room, swap meet, or entire estate. After you read some secrets and tips here and gain your "pickers' degree," you will be ready. You will find amazing, rare, and valuable treasures to keep, trade, or sell. Plus, you are going to have a whole lot of fun!

Pickers have been a hot topic on television and on the internet. As of this writing, there are almost 70 television programs being broadcast in the U.S., Canada, and the U.K. about pickers, collectors, and antiques.

TV shows like *American Pickers*, *Dealers*, and *Antiques Roadshow* all have a common theme. They talk about what they know about. They look for things that they have interest and knowledge about. I was at an *Antiques Roadshow* once, hauling my rare antique for a few hours in the long line of people to get into see these experts. What I discovered was that the reason the line is so long is because they need to see thousands of items before they come across something that the expert actually knows something about. I went home feeling cheated.

Before I wrote my first book, *Antique Secrets: How the Pickers Find Treasure in Another Man's Trash*, you could not even find much of anything in the literature about "pickers." What used to be a sub-culture is now in vogue and even famous. There is now a large army of pickers, hunters, foragers, and gatherers finding antiques and collectibles and items for resale. The competition is growing. Pickers glean from the fields of trash and junk beautiful and sometimes valuable treasures, and are hard working and sometimes clever experts in their fields of interest. They are constantly seeking and finding many types of interesting objects. They actually find many of the rare and historically important items we see in museums, as well as products you will see in fine antiques stores. These pickers also find many useful products as well. Some make a good living doing this. Pickers, as we describe in this book, have been gathering and reselling used things as an occupation forever. Sophisticated shoppers that spend large amounts at antiques stores and collectibles malls don't realize that there was a picker somewhere that found their items. It is the pickers who find and rescue much of what would have been lost forever in the dump. It's the pickers who help drive the interest and market for emerging collectibles.

This book will tell you how and why it's happening. As an observer, you will gain insight. As a participant, whether as a picker, collector, or dealer, it will assist you. Here are many wonderful tips, ideas, techniques, and secrets that you can try immediately.

Probably today more than ever before, picking is an important effort for these reasons:

1. The economy is uncertain and demanding people to find clever ways to supplement their incomes. Picking is a great way to receive extra income. When you go picking and then sell the items you find, it can be like another "fun" job, having a small business, and a profitable form of investing.

2. The world is full, and others who have lived are passing on, causing their wealth and worldly goods to be re-distributed. Pickers discover these things and aid in this re-distribution of goods.

3. People now more than ever in the world's history have more choices of objects. New, improved, and amazing things they feel they must have because marketing tells them they do. But guess what? There's not enough

room! So they sell, give, or donate the old stuff. This is good pickings for those with the knowledge and insight into the value of this disposed-of product. The secret is that old stuff tends to have more lasting value than the new, improved stuff. Early products were made in smaller quantities than the mass-produced stuff of today. Limited availability drives prices up. It's that supply and demand business. Besides, rare antique stuff when you find it is really fun!

4. Baby boomers are at the peak of their nostalgia cycle. They remember their old toys and other items. They remember their parents' and grandparents' stuff. They need to have that item they haven't seen in years. After all, they'll never find another one again, so what if it's ten times its original price—it's worth it. Pickers know this and feel it, too. The item jumps out at you, with its old lettering, heavy and well-built frame, or classic markings that give away the era.

5. Information is at its peak right now, and you can find it on all subjects. There are specialists in all areas of interests. The Internet is an amazing resource of information and history on every subject. At my last count, there were over 70 different television programs now that have to do with picking in some form. There is fervor in collecting, restoring, selling, and identifying. Pickers have more information on each and every type of product or item they seek or find.

6. Everything is collectible! It seems you can find a club or books on all subjects imaginable. You can specialize in anything. There are many places to find things in your area.

7. Recycling is important, whether you are an environmentalist or not. Recycling can make you money. Is that important? We will cover recycling in more detail in Chapter 1.

8. You will save on your expenditures. Because of the way I have been buying things for many years for pennies on the dollar, it has changed me and I have a difficult time buying anything at list price. You can get pretty creative when it comes to saving money. Cheapskate? Yeah.

I need to explain to you how and why this book was written. Throughout the book, you will see discussions, tips, and topics. These apply to pickers, collectors, and dealers. I almost combine and interchange the topics among all three viewpoints. I do this because I really believe that in most cases, people who are involved in this work or hobby are some sort of combination of the three.

This book is about my experiences, the experiences and opinions of many others, and my philosophy mixed in with technique. I wrote most of this book on the fly while it was happening. I saw, did, participated, and kept notes. I wrote about things that worked for me and also some failures. I also have

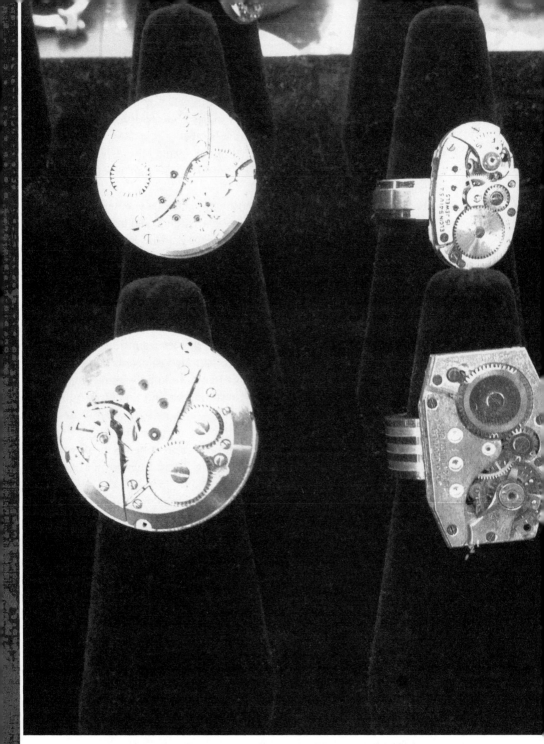

Thanks to steampunk, a subgenre of science fiction that typically features steam-powered machinery and has a setting inspired by industrialized Western civilization during the 19th century, there is a subculture of people who clamor for items that look like they were made in the steam age. This is a boon for pickers who now have a market for broken and obsolete items they find, including watch gears, like the ones here that have been fashioned into steampunk rings.

shared many proven secrets, tips, and ideas. There are many great methods discussed here to look for, find, get, and sell treasures of all kinds.

A collector has to obtain things to collect, so may go picking for items or buy from pickers and various dealers. He changes his interests occasionally and sells off items, becoming a dealer. The collector, who knows the ins and outs of the business, will assemble the finest collection and save money doing it.

The picker finds things he usually sells to dealers and collectors for profit. He may start to collect some of his finds, all the while growing, learning, and improving. He can become a collector, and because he is an expert in his specialty, he becomes a dealer for some things while still picking for other dealers and collectors.

A dealer may find it necessary to continue to pick in order to be profitable. It may be that he or she just continues to have some great sources still available. (If you have a great fishing hole, you use it!) Hopefully, the dealer has some collecting fervor to keep them enthusiastic about the business. The dealer, who understands collectors and their passions, can relate to them. The best dealers also know how pickers think, and know what is important to them. This is because they've been there. Besides, if she keeps her pickers happy, they will offer her the best products on a continuing basis.

Hopefully this will clear up some of the confusion. So just read, do, learn, and most of all have fun. You will be a better picker, collector, and dealer.

This has been a difficult book to write, but the subject matter isn't particularly difficult, and the secrets weren't too hard for me to tell. The biggest problem I've dealt with is how hard it is to break away from the actual picking.

It's fun, exciting, profitable, educating, and full of adventure. But on the other hand, I could not have been able to write the book without the actual experience of picking and dealing.

I have been a picker for most of my life. I discovered dumpster diving way before it was a fad, or to some, a lifestyle. I have had my own personal "college education," and several advanced engineering "degrees" from the piles of stuff I have taken apart, figured out, reversed engineered, and even sometimes fixed. I love technology, electronics, science, art, and natural sciences. My hobbies have included reading, optics and holography, mineralogy, antique radios, and many other types of antiques, both technical, and beautiful, and now, glass (hot, warm, and cold). I have found that people throw away, give away, trade, sell off, auction, and donate more boxes, piles, truckloads, and pallets of the stuff that fascinates me. There is not enough room to store it. I cannot by myself even sell it fast enough to make room for more.

THE PICKING BOOKS DEALERS DON'T WANT YOU TO KNOW ABOUT

When I wrote my first edition of this book, based on another book I wrote called *Antique Secrets: How the Pickers Find Treasure in Another Man's Trash*, I went to a local large antiques mall and showed it to the owner. I asked if they could sell some copies there. She looked through the book and started to get a little belligerent with me. She said, "I do not want any of my people or customers even knowing about this stuff." I asked her if she wanted a copy, but she was too mad and walked away. Imagine if she saw this edition of the book, which has new and expanded information.

Readers disagree with her, though, and one recently told me: *We have many books about antique glass and ceramics and other collectibles. I think that your local antiques dealer is very close-minded and short sighted. She doesn't realize that the more we all know, the more fine antiques and collectibles will be found by pickers and what we like to call book scouts. This seems to be an American way to reuse and recycle and to rescue rare collectors items from dumpsters and trash dumps. The antiques dealers that run these antiques malls for pickers and dealers should buy and provide these pickers each with a copy of the* Pickers Bible. *They will learn how to find more and better items for their cases and booths in the antiques mall. These individual people (thousands and thousands of them) are out there finding better items than what you see on* Pawn Stars, American Pickers *or* Auction Hunters *or* Storage Wars*!*

Besides, pickers find many items for resale in the actual antiques mall stores, too! Your dealer needs to embrace any and every way to educate their internal and external customers. I also think that a few enterprising estate sale companies should buy the Picker's Bible *and have them for sale at the checkout table. A large percentage of their customers are pickers and if they instruct them better, they spend more money. My main goal is to protect history by discovering more of our important antique heritage. Yeah, pickers!*

As a picker, I wish I was an accountant sometimes. Perhaps you could obtain a client that has an antiques mall. You could keep the books. You would also know which dealers in the mall are doing the best, and learn why they are so successful. You could get first look at stuff as it comes in. I am sure you could trade for items you want by helping some of the dealers with their accounting needs or consulting. If you were a real estate agent, it would be perfect. I know of estate sale companies that will set up for a weekend sale in a vacant home that is on the market, because they have a lot of inventory to sell off. They partner with the realtor, the realtor gets exposure by more people seeing the place, and everyone wins. If you are a good accountant, you are clever. Just look for opportunities and be resourceful. Good luck.

The trend of recycling and repurposing found objects into art and other products has also created a new market for pickers who come across any old and discarded items. Here, old golf clubs get new life as art pieces.

Antiques shows are prime places for pickers, both to find and sell stuff. Plus there is the major benefit of meeting great new contacts to find items.

Chapter 1

....

The Art of Picking

The first time I ever heard about the term "pickers" was from a collector I know. This was many years before the Internet was available. This collector had an entire basement filled with antique brass mining lamps. He also had walls loaded with miners' candlestick holders and other mining memorabilia. I asked him how he could possibly find so many fantastic pieces from around there. He laughed and told me of how he had pickers from all over the country send him pieces to buy. He said they went to places such as yard sales, antiques stores, and thrift shops looking for items to send him. He told me it was almost as if he had "hired" them to look for him. I had never heard of such a thing. I was intrigued and had to know more. He said that these pickers knew about this particular collectible and knew he would pay good prices for the better pieces. He told me there were pickers for almost any type of collectible. His pickers had a good captive customer (him) and thus he had an endless supply of good items.

The next time I heard the term "picker," I was waiting in line in a library book sale. The old timer in front of me was explaining how he had to get there early in order to get in front of all the "book pickers" (also known as book scouts). There was that term again. He described how some of the big book dealers had hired pickers to find certain titles for them.

This amazed me. You mean that collectors, antiques dealers, and book-stores buy from a group or subculture of people called pickers? Exactly. Just about anyone who wants to can go picking and then bring the items to these dealers and sell them at the back door. The fact is, the majority of the inventory that many dealers have originated from the front lines of picking. What you see in an antiques store or a museum is an assemblage of items. It didn't just happen. It was built over many years of gathering, finding, trading, and collecting. It was all harvested.

Think of the word picking or "to pick." Have you ever said, "Look what I just picked up" or "Boy, it was slim pickings today?" We've heard of berry pickers, stock pickers, fruit pickers, and rag pickers, even a miner's pick. These are all terms for harvesting, aren't they? Antiques and collectibles pickers are, in fact, harvesters.

My old-timer friend in line at the book sale spoke with a little resentment toward the pickers. What he didn't admit was that even a collector such as himself was there to pick for himself.

Sometimes there is a perception that because something found its way to a thrift store or a yard sale it must be worthless, dirty, or just a doggy type of thing. The other perception is that if it is in an antiques store, it must be a rare and precious thing. I want to tell you that those rare and precious things are found in dingy, dirty, and cluttered places and brought to light and rescued many times by pickers.

The picker used to be perceived by some as a dirty scrounger; however, the picker is an artist and a professional. Television shows have done much to raise the picker from scrounger to artist. I know of all sorts of pickers. Some have excellent jobs and just pick part-time. Others pick full-time. There are those who pick just to stay alive. Some are destitute and homeless, while others have successful stores and businesses.

I know of doctors, corporate officers, and other professionals who pick during their lunch hours and days off—you don't need to quit your job to do this.

There are also the obsessed collectors who just have to pick. Some are just fixer-uppers or do-it-yourselfers. Many pickers supplement their incomes by scouting for dealers. Some antiques dealers pick for their own store whenever they have time.

Picking ought to be thought more of as a profession; after all, it is more of an art than it is a labor. Good picking is a talent. Picking is a great hobby or even a vocation for some, as well as being a lucrative business for others. It might be a pastime, a livelihood, or sport. Whatever the individual's reason, it can be enjoyable and fun. It's a blast!

Have you ever bought an item for $5 and sold it the same day for $100? I have. I've bought many items for several dollars and sold for thousands of dollars. Pickers do it all the time. Have you wondered how in the world antiques shops get so much stuff? Where do they find it all? Have you ever declared, "My grandmother had one of those?" Don't you wish you had it today?

Welcome to the world of the professional picker. You are, can, and should be collecting and picking for antiques, collectibles, and other stuff. This book contains secrets, tips, thoughts, and experiences that will really help you, guide you, and professionalize what you do.

When I was quite young, I remember going behind the neighborhood stores and businesses and finding lots of fun and interesting junk. Now it seems that dumpster diving is reserved for the truly despondent. When I did it, it was just for fun. Picking is truly an honorable profession, even though you get some deals that may seem to be so unbelievable that it may look otherwise.

Picking has been kind of a natural thing for me for some reason. As a boy, I remember gathering old pop bottles and car batteries to trade in for cash. I used to take apart electronic and electrical products and sell the scrap copper. I've found old TVs and radios. I even remember selling an antique wind-up mantle clock to a dealer for $5.

I was always attracted to surplus and thrift stores. I'd talk to people about my hobby and the next thing you knew, they would bring something over to give me. I also collected stamps and coins as a child, which gave me a little organization and structure as a true collector. That didn't prevent me from searching out free items. In a dumpster behind a neighborhood drugstore, I found store fixtures and displays that really looked cool in my room. I used to bring armfuls of half-full bottles of perfume demonstrators that I would give to my delighted mother. I'd get all sorts of little junk that pleased my friends and myself. Lots of good trade stock!

In a dumpster behind a gift distributor, I found boxes of postcards and greeting cards. Down by the car wash, they had a hill out back where they dumped out the stuff they vacuumed from cars and I remember finding many quarters, nickels, dimes, jewelry, and even stuff like old stock certificates.

I remember having neighbors let me go through piles of junk and garages of stuff just before they moved or when someone died, and finding trinkets, antique clocks, and radios that I'd swap, sell, or experiment with. We even had a guy my brother worked for who called up my father and said he needed to leave town because the mob was after him. He said we could have anything in the house we wanted.

A variety of tins at an antiques show. Cases with small items like this can hold a lot of things, and also get a lot of attention.

Since my adult neighbors and friends knew I was interested in old keys, science, and electronics, when junk was thrown out, they threw it my way. Curbside spring cleaning piles used to be a lot better when I was a boy, too, as people tossed away their stuff.

I was indeed a picker, but just didn't know the activity had a name for it.

Later on in my life, I got interested in collecting rocks and minerals. I collected literally tons of material—even many museum-quality specimens. I loved to go prospecting. I'm kind of an old miner. Because I was a picker of sorts from early in my childhood, it has helped me to be a better prospector now. I truly feel and think, while I am out picking, that I am on a field trip.

My early adventures in picking were literally like hunting for and finding treasure. The excitement, the hoarding, and the organization of what I found helped me in other areas. As I worked on prospecting skills, I would research the literature—this paid off, as did leads and hunches.

Friends were also helpful. All of the digging, trying, and searching taught me that if you think, work, want, keep going, and believe—it really pays off! The more you prospect, the more you find.

In rocks, junk, or antiques, I realized that to find the treasure, you just have to dig a little bit more. Sometimes it's just a bit more in the same area and just inches away. You have to read the terrain and look for slight hints and telltale signs that are an indication of the valuable ore. You need to study all of the literature, watch for trends, and listen well.

All of this experience gave me what I really needed to be a more successful picker. The habits and experience, passion, belief and goals, combined with absolute interest and joy, all develop what is called a "knack." You'll get a knack for it. After reading this book and trying the things described here, you will be way ahead in the profession of picking.

SOME GREAT DEALS I'VE FOUND

At the first auction I ever attended, I was both impressed and fascinated... and I blew it. Some optical grinders came up for bid and I couldn't believe how quick the sale happened. It was over before I even discovered I wanted one of them. There were six machines in the lot that were interesting pieces of equipment. You could take a pattern of any size and shape, and these grinders would copy the pattern by grinding the glass to the shape. They had a large diamond grinding wheel, and all of the fancy electronic controls to do a precise job. The entire lot was bid and sold for $60. After the auction, I searched for the winning bidder. I talked him into selling me one unit for $60, the amount he paid for the lot. I got it home, figured out how it worked, and played with it for a while. Ultimately, I sold it to a company that made glass holograms into jewelry for $1,100. This gave me the cash to go buy my first personal computer.

At another auction, I bought a hot stamp printer for $25. These are used to imprint monograms on everything from stationary to napkins. Incidentally, my purchase was from someone else who bid on the item, when he realized he didn't have a use for it. I later sold the machine to a local bookstore for $200 in cash and an additional $200 in trade. Since then, I have picked up and moved more of these machines. I learned what they were worth, and use that knowledge later.

Once I bought a large wood display case with sliding glass doors for $100. It also had four drawers under the doors. When I got the thing loaded up and home, I discovered the drawers were stuffed with electronic parts and products. I sold just the contents of the drawers I found for $150.

One day I purchased two old, new-in-the-box electron tubes for $25 a piece. It so happened these were some rare and sought-after audio tubes and I sold them three days later for $350 each. One week later, I took the profit I made from the tubes and bought a rare antique radio, which is worth many times more than what I paid for it.

In a thrift store once, I found several boxes (500 pieces per box) of small electronic parts. I knew where and how the parts were used, so I contacted a supplier who dealt in the same brand of parts. I ultimately traded the lot for a new portable video camera. I was out a total of about $45.

HOW PICKERS CAN MAKE MONEY

You might be wondering how the public perceives us pickers. Well, it's rather like lawyers, used car salesmen, and auto mechanics. Either you are loved and appreciated or you're despised. My hope by writing this book is to change any negative reputation of pickers. Even the famous pickers you see on television shows have controversy surrounding them. If you make too much on a deal, then you are taking advantage of people in some eyes. To others, you are quite savvy, and they want to do some deals like you, emulating the negotiation skills they see. This is, after all, a full-time job and career for some. This could be a profession, too—if you act as a professional.

The picker does a service, and has rescued many important and historic relics, antiques, artwork, and fine furniture. The picker supplies businesses with product to sell. The picker finds sought-after merchandise for those with needs and wants that would be impossible otherwise. Broken pieces are replaced. Lost volumes fill voids in sets of needed libraries. Historical information is assembled more completely and accurately because of the picker. Beautiful classic antiques find the proper destinations to those who now enjoy them. Value is added to otherwise useless junk. The picker actually perfected the recycling industry that is so important to certain groups and individuals, now, only decades ago!

The picker makes a living and is not afraid to work hard. The picker can be an excellent resource and consultant with in-depth knowledge on products, markets, and trends. Why does the picker sometimes get a bad rap? Or what can you as a picker do to clean up your act and get the respect you may deserve?

Q: Aren't thrift stores, yard sales, and swap meets kind of a grungy and somewhat dirty environment?
A: Don't worry about it. The professional steelworker, plumber, and even doctors and dentists work in and around stuff I'd have a hard time touching.

Q: What about rudeness? It seems as if pickers are willing to push you out of the way when you're looking at something they are interested in. Some pickers are downright abusive.
A: Here's one complaint I hear the most: some pickers knock you over

PACKRATS AND HOARDERS

Are you one of those people who could be called a packrat? Are you afraid your home will be on television one day as a hoarder's? You will know if you answer yes to any of these, and especially all: Do you save stuff because it might be valuable one day or because you never know when you might need it? Do you love to rummage through grandma's attic, or search thrift stores, old hardware, and junk stores for treasure? Do piles of junk look like a gold mine to you? Do you frequent swap meets and buy, trade, or even sell stuff often? Do you slam on your brakes, make U-turns, and park funny just because you saw a yard sale? Does your heart start to beat fast when you go to an estate sale or an auction?

if there is good stuff and lots of competition. There is a lot of difference between grabbing and quickly picking something up. Stripping shelves is mean. It is a bad idea many times economically, because you can be left with unsold junk yourself. Don't be greedy and push others.

Q: What about early birds?
A: I have to admit, the early bird does get the good stuff. Just be cool, kind, and polite. If you're first in line don't be obnoxious. Being the early bird is one thing, but some people just wait around (especially thrift stores), almost living there. This gives pickers a bad name. The early bird gets a worm and moves on. If that bird is a vulture and circles until its prey is dead, it usually stinks, too. I do know people who show up a day early and play dumb, saying, "I thought the sale was today." Several times they do get in, and hi-grade the sale.

Q: What about snakes, cheats, and thieves?
A: Don't do it. Be fair and honest—it will pay off. There are enough good deals out there for everyone. Enjoy the good deals when they come along, but don't make one, if it doesn't exist, by being dishonest.

Q: They are a bunch of cheapskates!

A: Well, the deal has to be profitable in order for anyone to buy it. The pickers see so much of the same product over and over that they get a good feel for what something sells for. If someone tries to sell an item at retail price or higher, a good picker will either walk on past the item or at least try to inform the seller of what they know about the item they are trying to sell. It could be out of the kindness of your heart, which could find you a good friend and maybe future contact. You might even find it turns into a form of negotiation, and you may just end up with it.

Q: What about competition? Isn't it pretty fierce?

A: There may be competitors out there but that constant supply and demand is what creates this economy that is interested in what you find. Besides, there always seems to be a different interest and taste for every picker and dealer out there. The variety available is truly unbelievable. The abundance is also hard to believe once you are out there. Pickers buy from other pickers. Because of the different contacts and the different experiences we all have, the value varies considerably. You could buy an item at an antiques store at its listed retail price because you know what a particular collector or another dealer will pay for it. It really depends on who and what you know.(And, what the other guy does not know…)

Q: Don't antique dealers consider pickers just a necessary evil?

A: Not so. I know dealers who love to see their picker come in. They share in the excitement of the find and profit greatly, too. I have heard the term friend used often as pickers refer to their dealers. This whole thing is a win-win situation we are discussing anyway. I think the pickers who dealers dislike are the ones who come in their store never buying or selling, only looking at the prices so they can know what their finds might retail at. If you have a great first-name relationship with your dealers, you have ready customers awaiting your find and your inventory turns quickly. This means PROFIT!

Some pickers, I'm sure, generally feel they don't receive any respect. They might feel people think they are crazy or are a scrounger, or call them a packrat or make other comments. We absolutely love to laugh at those cracks all the way to the bank.

There are some who laugh when they learn about what you find on a search. In one instance, the same folks who laughed about a recent purchase made a trip to one of my haunts and didn't find a thing. They wrongly believe you can go one time and find exactly what you are looking for. Ot/ the same people might ask, "Hey, can you look for such and such an item when you're out scrounging?" (Oh, so now I'm a resource!)

THE HAPPY PICKER

Pickers come from all sorts of backgrounds, and have many reasons for picking. For example, some people pick:

AS EMPLOYMENT: Some make their entire living picking. It might be from desperation, lack of work, or preference. Several pickers I have spoken to don't want the regular "8 to 5 job." In many cases, the annual income of picking beats what a 9 to 5 job brings in.

AS A HOBBY: It might be that you are just a collector. I got into it as a moneymaking hobby, and started as just a way to improve my collection and found a larger world inside with some interesting opportunities. I still keep the finest pieces for my collection—that is, usually, until something better comes along. Some do it because they love the history and the antiquarian aspects of it all. It's always good to have historical information and experience. This is a big benefit to those who pick, just as a scientific and engineering background can help you identify valuable items in more obscure fields. I love to study the history of items I am finding.

INVESTORS: There are some who also consider what they do as an investment. They probably get a better return on their investment than if the money was in the stock market, but as with any investment, you can still be stung and lose your shirt.

AS A BUSINESS: This can be in the form of a dealer, a broker, a shop owner, or just wholesaling what you find to dealers and collectors. You could also include people with many years of experience, who do appraising and consulting.

I spoke to a dealer at a weekly fairground swap meet, which offers large buildings that house dealers. It so happens that the dealers have a semi-permanent location for their store during most of the year. This swap meet is open for selling on weekends only. As we spoke, I asked him about his operation. It turns out that one particular dealer picks during the week, replenishes his stock, then sells all weekend. He estimates he clears $80,000 a year.

I've met others making similar amounts, and dealers who say they hire part-time pickers who easily do $30,000 per year. He says they only go out on weekends to do so. He buys everything from them on Monday.

I know a smart picker/businessman who does very well because of his hard work. He advertises in more than 30 national publications, certain niche magazines that he targets with display ads and classified ads listing his wants, and even has a toll-free number. He probably makes twice what I do in my "real job." He also has a large warehouse space to hold and sort his finds. He will attend several trade shows during the year to sell, but more importantly, to gain exposure. These shows are usually esoteric and specific swap meets pertaining to his field. When he attends a show, he will buy and sell "all the way there" and "all the way back" as he drives with his inventory. He may only sell $2,000 out of his show booth, but pre-sell and deliver at the show $10,000. Another $10,000 may be sold on his drive to the show, or on his way back home, delivering pre-sold items to his good contacts. Plus, he now has money to purchase items on the way back, too.

He will also sell many large lots of inventory to dealers who visit these shows as part of their annual buying trips. They know him because of the exposure through shows and from his advertising. His ads just state "WANTED" never "For sale." His regular customers know he wants certain items for one purpose: to sell it to someone else.

For the right person, it can be fun; in fact, so much fun you don't realize work is involved. However, it's not always an easy job. There is stiff, aggressive, and sometimes unfair competition. There's usually much driving, which burns up gasoline and puts wear and tear on your vehicle. There is a signifi-

Some neat finds at a San Jose Flea Market.

cant time devoted to seeking, obtaining, sorting, cleaning, fixing, and selling your finds. Sometimes it's a dirty job. Sometimes it's very heavy.

Other skills needed to set you apart from other pickers include listening, bargaining, researching, and knowing where to find good information. Even just loving to shop helps you rise above your competition. My wife likes to go to estate sales with me, calling it her "fix" of yard sailing. If you are an artist or have a good eye for beauty and aesthetics, you'll have a skill many don't have. If you love to fix things and have certain craft skills, you may get more for the stuff you find. Remember, those who are goal-oriented always come out on top. Hopefully you'll also have some good business sense.

PICKER, DEALER, COLLECTOR—OR ALL THREE?

Some might argue that you can't be a picker, a collector, and a dealer at the same time. I disagree. True, if you have a hard time parting with the best items, you might not have the most cash flow, but a dealer who also collects has a finer sense of what a collector wants. A collector who deals can constantly improve his or her collection. A picker does not just need to be mercenary, that is, only in it for the money. A picker can do very well collecting and selling, too. There are all kinds of fine lines between these terms. The ratio might be completely different for each individual, but wearing various hats, I believe, is healthy. It's unhealthy for a dealer to resent all collectors because of their peculiarities or for a collector to resent all dealers because of their money-grubbing tendencies.

We collectors need to thank dealers for the wonderful items they bring to the market. Otherwise we would have little to collect. We dealers need to love the collectors, bless their hearts, for providing demand for our inventory. The whole law economy is based upon supply (dealers and pickers) and demand (collectors). If you take all of the titles away, this whole thing is about finding, moving, studying, improving, discovering, enjoying, and investing.

I once had an ongoing argument with a dealer who refused to admit he collected anything for himself. He said everything was for sale. He always sold good items and expensive items. He was a successful businessman because he was organized and made a beautiful display of his goods. As a collector, I didn't buy much from him. It was all money to him. I did buy many items from many other dealers that were also collectors. I think I did better because they would also trade with me. By being collectors, too, I guess I felt they could relate.

I've asked a few others—even large dealers—if they collect. It has been refreshing and interesting to find that many do. I also learn what their interests and passions are. Who knows, maybe just knowing this will help me in future deals with them.

PERKS AND FRINGE BENEFITS

We've all seen the books, junk mail, and the articles and ads promising, "Buy at wholesale—20 percent to 40 percent off!" First of all, if you buy low and sell for a good profit, your income improves. Also, as you buy items for yourself at yard sale prices (typically a dime or less on the dollar), your purchasing power is magnified. Now, if you buy at a low price and then trade it for its market price for an item you want or need, this also enhances your dollar. This is better than the promises of buying wholesale.

Here is a good example: I was given a large oak cabinet that I thought would look appropriate in an antiques store. I took a photo of the cabinet into the first likely store and the owner said she was interested. I hauled it over in a borrowed truck. She let me pick out anything in the store I wanted up to a value of $200. Kind of a little shopping spree! I picked out an item or two and one was marked $90. This item turned out to have a value of a couple hundred dollars more after I got it home and did some research on it.

It's wonderful to buy stuff at a penny or even a dime on the dollar. Almost as fun as selling things at multiple times what I paid for them.

LIFESTYLES OF THE RICH AND LUCKY

This book is about doubling your income or more. It's about raising your standard of living. You not only make more income in buying and selling at a great profit, you also have much more money up front. When you are out picking for items in your particular line of goods, you also find many items you can use. The prices you find these needed items for are way below the regular or list price. So if you buy a mountain bike for $15 or a $500 rooftop evaporative cooler for $50 as I did, you're virtually living at a higher standard of living than your income would normally allow. One time I found a nice chain saw for $25. I find useful tools, expensive scientific equipment, and furniture for my wife. I look for all sorts of useful stuff out of my regular specialty.

This is all in addition to the extra living you are making now by picking. You are living beyond your means but staying within your budget. Plus, it is so fun!

PICKERS WERE THE FIRST RECYCLERS

One of the great benefits of all of this effort is all of the recycling that is being done. It's been this way forever. Pickers, for years, have been rescuing items from being wasted and turning them into items that are now cherished.

As you rescue items from the landfill, you are doing a great service not only to the recycling effort, but finding things that are valuable and interesting.

I've even heard stories of certain thrift shops setting up free zones where people can drop off certain items and others can take what they need; things that can be used, like canning jars and certain other useful items. You also

RECYCLING HAS GROWN IN MANY DIFFERENT DIRECTIONS

Look up these terms online and you will find all sorts of great ideas:

FREECYCLING: giving it to others to use.

HACKERS AND MAKERS AND DO IT YOURSELF: take apart, figure it out, and make something else.

RECLAIMED: see all of these subjects.

RECYCLING: rescuing before it's trash.

REDUCE: living on less, using what you have.

REFINING: recovering the precious metals.

REPURPOSING: creative recycling, art, etc.

RESTORED: fixing it up like new.

REUSED: find another new use instead of trash.

SALVAGED: tearing down and reselling.

SCRAPPED: rescuing the metals from the trash.

SHABBY CHIC: something old used to decorate.

STEAMPUNK: high tech meets old fashioned, crazy use of old things with new tech.

SURPLUS: reselling of excess and obsolete.

UPCYCLED: making something from scrap items, crafts, jewelry, etc.

might check with your local waste disposal agency for items. I am aware of a municipal hazardous waste disposal site that has a free store set up. Here residents can drop off all of their leftover paint, insecticides, and chemicals for proper disposal. They have this store stocked with near-full or even new containers of these items. You can go in and take all of the stuff you might need for free, including good bug spray, paint for your house, or other items.

DON'T BE DISCOURAGED

Discouragement is a killer in this business. It's when you see another picker or collector hauling his armload out just before you arrive on the scene that can really be disheartening. Just about as bad is not buying an item when you probably should have and returning later to find it's gone. I had a bad experience once where I noticed a small obscure ad in the newspaper classifieds for an "Old Victrola" for $200 or best offer. I called and the daughter of the house was there alone. She had no idea if it was sold yet. She described it as being about four feet high, all mahogany, with an inside lid that said Edison. It also had about 30 thick records in the bottom cabinet. She said all it needed was a needle. The dad worked nights and I couldn't call until the next day. It was late, but I asked if her mother would be home later and if it was okay to call even then. She agreed and I did. The mom said it was still available and to come over. So I went over and the mom was on a portable phone talking to the dad, who told her he had already agreed to sell it to a dealer who was picking it up the next day. Man, I hate it when that happens. I looked at the machine and it was flawless.

What you have to keep reminding yourself is:

1. You still have your money.
2. Other deals will definitely come your way.
3. This is proof that you're on the right track, a little late maybe, but on the right track, nonetheless.
4. You are learning. Besides, it's better than staying still.
5. Don't dwell on the bad deals. If you want, make a list of the stupid things you do or the sour deals. Now you have a place to store those stories and don't have to worry about them. After all, it makes great conversation. I personally have a long list of regrets. Usually when I "put the problem on my pile of regrets" it is somehow therapeutic.

License plates have been recycled into birdhouses.

Long-forgotten dolls have been repurposed into clocks and other objects that may be a little creepy, but are still cool.

A PICKER'S PILE OF REGRETS

I can vividly remember the ones that got away. There have been many times I was hunting for antiques and hesitated, just did not have the cash, or talked myself out of a good deal, only to find out later what a dummy I was. I was recently behind one of my competition buddies in an estate sale. The ad said they had antique cameras. I actually saw the antique cameras after my friend. There was a box with a vintage Leica and a bunch of lenses, accessories, and literature. They had it marked $700. I commented to the dealer about the price. He said, "Yeah, punch it up" (look online), then blurted out some prices. I walked away, asked my buddy, "Did you see the Leica?" "Yeah," he said, "$700 is too much for me." So I felt my decision was good, but I found out later that day that he just walked up to the dealer asked, "What's the least you'd take?" He said, "$550." My buddy bought it. Gosh, I would have paid $550!

What happened here is, I was one of the regular buyers the dealer knew, and so was my friend. We and everybody else were passing on the camera. The sale continued on with no purchase at $700. My asking was not a negotiating question. My friend's asking WAS a negotiating question. So the dealer probably decided quickly that he needed to make the sale and sold it to my friend. It would normally go for about $2,000 on eBay. He got $1,500.

I could have had this Leica camera and all the lenses and accessories for $550, but I delayed. The person who bought it sold it on eBay for $1,500.

I beat myself up about these regrets, so I've decided to just put them all on my "picker pile" with all the others that went south. It's now just a pile. I learned, and now I've taught you.

You'll know when you are starting to do well at picking. First your neighbors will show some astonishment and jealousies often at some of the absolute luck you have in finding good stuff. You may even hear from a fellow picker, something like, "Ivan and I were talking and we have to admit, you're finding an awful lot of good stuff. You are a pretty good picker." Your head starts to swell, etc., but you can get discouraged even while at your best. How? It's called "being in the right place at the wrong time."

You'll know when it's going good. You have your favorite haunts to check out. You have a good schedule. You have found good stuff there before. Your system for quickly moving and eyeing the areas works perfectly, and you don't miss much. It works and it's proven. Then it happens … in the hands of your competition, which could be a fellow picker, or just a common shopper, is the prize of the day. If you had started in that place when you entered the store that day, the item would have been yours. You may just want to sit right down on the floor and cry, but think of the great fishermen with stories of the one that got away, the big sports heroes and their mighty defeats, or the great salesmen who were a nickel too high in their price and lost the million-dollar bid.

It just means that yes, you are on the right track and finding good stuff. Your time will come to get it. Never quit.

KNOW WHEN TO KEEP QUIET

Sometimes in excitement, I've bragged about what I've recently found and maybe where I found it, and even how much I paid for it. This can be stupid. I did this once to a fellow I was trading with at a specialized swap meet. I told him exuberantly where and how I found the particular piece he was trading for, and it only cost so much, and blah, blah, blah. Now I see the guy go to that place we talked about all the time. I had never seen him there before that conversation, and now I wonder what he's been finding there when I'm not around. I've especially been tempted to tell other pickers to keep an eye out for a certain pre-collectible for me, which happens to be a good cash maker right now, but I don't tell. I can still find them; they are still only a dollar or two apiece instead of "list" price.

Don't brag, keep it to yourself; you'll be better off. If you simply have to say something to someone, find a confidant who won't stick you in the back. On the other hand, LISTEN. People love to brag about their stuff, their finds, and will GIVE you all sorts of good information. You will hear things while waiting in line to go into an estate sale that can be valuable. You can follow fellow pickers out to their car after they bought items. They will tell you stuff, sell you stuff, and you can really win some great information.

THE ETHICS OF PICKING

So I found a good deal once. I mean a really good deal. One of those once-in-a-lifetime or at least once-a-year-or-two deals. It was a good price. But was I unethical? For example, if I pay $5 for an item and turn it over tomorrow for $200, this is unbelievable profit margin. Did I take advantage of the seller? Did I take advantage of the person who pays me $200? Am I a terrible person?

These are some good questions. Let's look at some possible answers or at least try to rationalize, or you just might go crazy and maybe feel bad about what you are doing with all this stuff.

I go traveling in the desert and find a gold nugget. It's big, pure, and beautiful and feels heavy. It was put there by nature and this is the first time man has ever seen it. It is a one-ounce beautiful, clean nugget. I paid nothing for it except for gasoline to get to the site. This gold nugget has value. I could get close to $1,500 to $2,000 or more for it. Did I take advantage of anyone? Should I pay someone for it? It was found on public land. Should I give a large discount to the buyer because, after all, I didn't have to pay anything for it?

If someone gives me an antique and I sell it for $500, do I take advantage of the giver or the buyer? If I find that same antique in a thrift store or at an estate sale with a price sticker of $5 and sell it for the same $500, am I taking advantage of anyone? Is this immoral? Or am I just a good investor? I really did buy something for $5 and sell it for $500. The buyer may know how much I paid for it and was pleased to pay the $500. To him, this was a bargain.

As a prospector, I studied literature on the terrain and looked for certain geologic features to find the gold nugget. I traveled the desert twenty or thirty times before to see if I could find the lode. As a picker, I also studied my specialty in the antiques field, read books I paid money for, and I made several purchases before the big profitable find that were poor investments. This time and studying, along with the trial and error, creates knowledge that has to count for something.

I invested money and time to learn about it.

I invested time to go find it.

I invested energy to get it.

I invested the funds to procure it.

I invested effort to clean, repair, restore, and display it.

I invested study and time to find customers for it. I work to move it. I invested experience and knowledge of how to find it.

I invested the risk, knowing full well it might not sell or might sell at a loss eventually.

Plus, I may have a warehouse full of junk that I cannot sell for a profit, and may need to give away someday.

This is an education we're talking about. It's years of experience, effort, study, investment, and risk. It is the same if you are a doctor, contractor, business professional, or a retail merchant. Your efforts must be worth it. The fee, bid, service charge, or profit is your pay for a job well done.

What about the idea that you are making money off others' misfortunes? An estate sale occurs because someone died. Many moving sales may happen because of a divorce. Isn't this a terrible thing to do? It used to really bother me to think about all of this.

One day I was helping a newly divorced lady out of her home. We were putting her belongings into a large trailer, which was getting full with the items she really wanted to take. She also threw away many usable items. The largest and best of those she didn't want went to a local thrift store. Now, I know the thrift store was not taking advantage of her. The thrift store is a *solution* to this woman, as well as many others.

Doctors make their living from people who are sick. Lawyers depend on people who are in trouble to further their career. Firemen exist because of damage. Police, funeral directors, and news people all do the same. Doctors are a *solution* for the pain. Lawyers correct and justify trouble. We all live and do the same. Humans are the only species who survive by serving others.

You are not stealing (at least I hope you're not) when you buy and clean out a deceased person's house. You're not vultures when you sort through some deceased person's belongings—you are a *solution* for the estate.

When I finished with a big brokering deal I put together, I learned a lot about stewardship and value added. I wondered about the pricing of the estate, the profit the dealer would make, and about my dealings. Was this all done correctly and honestly? I really believe if you are ethical, you'll do better in this business than those who aren't. Honesty pays off. The Golden Rule is still in effect. Making a profit is in itself not bad or wrong, but taking advantage of someone and stealing is bad.

So, what if the dealer bought a lot of stuff for $1,000 cash and ends up selling the lot for $2,000, or even $5,000? Is it OK to double the money, but not more? What if the seller names a price, but it's way below what the buyer was ready to pay?

You will find endless ethical questions in this business or I guess in any business.

First let's touch on stewardship (more discussed later). When I have an item, it's my property and I paid for it. I have stewardship. It's mine to use, dispose of, break, give away, or sell. I have ownership and I have a responsibility of its use. If I sell it, my stewardship is gone. If I die, my stewardship passes to someone else. I can't do anything again with the item. I've had my turn.

If an estate has legal claim on the item, it is now their stewardship. If they turn the sale or disposal to someone, that person has stewardship. If I buy it, I get to play with it next—you can't take it with you.

Now let's talk about value added.

Let's take the items that sold for $1,000 we mentioned above. The worth or value at this time they were sold is $1,000. That's it; that is what the seller got, and therefore is the value.

"But the seller could have received more if he would have asked for more?" This is true, but he didn't. For whatever reasons, decisions that were made during the transaction, side deals, pressures, thoughts, or feelings, the deal went for $1,000.

"But the dealer is going to make a $4,000 profit!"

This is true, but look at what is involved. (Think value added.)

The dealer has overhead. The dealer or buyer may have to transport it across several states. This might require shipping or renting a truck and spending money on removal, packing, and protecting. The dealer or buyer has to know about the stuff. He has spent years studying about it, reading, inspecting, gaining experience, and knowledge.

The dealer or buyer has the contacts and ready customers he has built up over time. He may have to clean or repair it, or restore it by removing damaging modifications using products he has on hand. He/she may have to go into debt to finance this buy, spend hundreds of hours, pay for labor to process the items. (Does the seller have to spend the time?)

The dealer or buyer may have to buy the bad and unsalable items along with the good, catalog, sort, test the product, and advertise. He/she may have to take it to specialized shows or sales to dispose of it, place it in a store and display it, or even pay for a rental storage space to warehouse it until sold.

VALUE-ADDED LESSON

The value of something is what you can or will take the time, energy, and effort to sell it for. The value to another person is what they can sell it for. As a seller, you have a lot of product to liquidate into cash. Here are the options:

1. Show it to a potential buyer who will take it all wholesale. (This is the quickest sale = 10 cents on the dollar.)

2. You can sort, fix, clean, display, price, and show it to many individuals at estate sales, yard sales, swap meets, etc. (A fairly quick sale except for your labor = 25 cents on the dollar.)

3. You could take it to various dealers at their businesses; taking particular lots they have interest in and wholesale it to them. (More time and money = 50 cents on the dollar.)

4. You can open a shop, display it, mail order it, and sell it to the public retail. (This process is a long sale, with lots of time and other expenses involved = full dollar.)

Watch gears are turned into steampunk creations. Steampunk takes repurposing to a higher and artsier level.

CHALLENGES AND PROBLEMS

Picking can be an exciting and fun venture. You can be successful and have a rewarding and fulfilling experience. But this list shows there are indeed pitfalls to picking, as well as any new business. You need to understand these things, going in with your eyes open.

- Bad checks
- Bad credit
- Bad deals or trades
- Bad ideas
- Bad investments
- Bad leads and bad information
- Bad stuff
- Being taken advantage of
- Breakage
- Burn out, lack of interest
- Business failure
- Changed minds
- Competition bought first
- Competition sold to customer first
- Debt and cash poor
- Delay in buying
- Disasters, fire, water, earthquake, damage
- Dishonesty
- Fears
- Getting scooped
- Greed
- Hi-grades vs. junk
- Injury (back aches, etc.)
- Lack of knowledge on products, pricing, etc.
- Overwhelmed
- Poor decisions
- Poor management
- Shattered dreams and hopes
- Shipping losses/damages
- Stupidity
- The economy
- Theft, vandalism, burglary
- Too late
- Too little time
- Too much stuff and no room
- Unhappy, dissatisfied customers, and refunds

SOUR DEALS HAPPEN

You get a call. The deal you made last week went bad. He wants his stuff back or money returned. The deal went south! Garbage! You feel bad, you're mad, and you're worried, for now you may have cash problems. You have that yucky tight nauseous knot in the pit of your stomach. Stuff happens.

Sometimes you can re-negotiate. If you quickly decide what the deal is worth to you at a lower level, you may be able to rescue it right now. You may be able to throw in something extra to satisfy him. Hopefully, as you keep talking and realize what the problem is, you may find a solution that helps both of you.

Sometimes the person is one who doesn't listen to reason and nothing you say or do makes a difference. Sometimes they may have a money problem, spouse problem, or something else that prevents them from going on.

But remember this: You will get over it. You are smarter now and will be more cautious in the future with this person. This is part of the picker education you are paying for. Your stuff still has the value it did before this deal. You'll sell it again. If it was your cash you got back, you at least still have the money. The next deal might even be better. Climb right back on the horse when you fall off. Go work on a completely different deal. Hopefully this will turn out positively and put this one way behind you and in perspective. Sometimes a knock on the side of your head like this really starts you thinking. Just as competition, it's a pain and you hate it and complain about it, but it makes you better and stronger. Overcoming a bad deal and turning it around, though painful, will make you better off than if you didn't have the experience. Keep your cool, tell them what you think, but don't let anger overtake you. Don't burn your bridges. It's just stuff after all.

GROWING PAINS

As the antiques and collectibles market matures, you see signs of growing pains. I've heard dealers complain recently of how bad it's getting with all of the buyers and collectors, including how they require everything in new or "in box" condition, and they are too aware or savvy.

Let's turn it around…

It used to be more common to find better deals at thrift stores or from dealers at swap meets, etc. Sellers are considered dealers and ask for higher prices. The dealers use price guides to price everything—the end result being that swap meets are turning into nomadic antiques stores.

I was in an antiques store where the dealer used the old price guide with lower prices when he wanted to buy from you, and would offer half of the listed price. He would then pull out the new price guide with higher prices to price something you wanted to buy. He was pretty smooth about how he did it and I'm sure most people didn't realize what he was doing. To me, though, it was obvious. Now with eBay, people will even print out a page of a listed

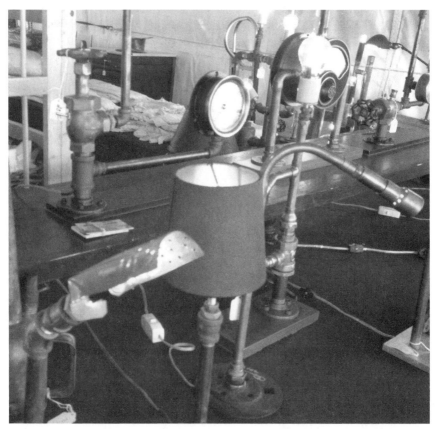

Steampunk lamps made out of fixtures and pipes. Pickers can now find a market for defunct broken and obsolete objects, but these items need to look cool.

item that is similar to what they are selling. You need to be careful here. First of all, you know they printed off the item they found with the highest price. Next, this is what it is *selling* for, not a completed item price. Get out your smart phone, and show them the truth.

QUIT SHOOTING YOUR MOUTH OFF

It's poor form to brag, and it can also get you into trouble because you might give away your secrets. Other dangers are that you might reveal your customers, vendors, or profit margin. Some people who are constantly boasting also reveal a clue to their intelligence, which could backfire on them.

Sometimes you might have a great deal you pulled off that has a fantastic story you just have to tell, but you end up finding that the story just upsets others, making them feel bad or jealous, when you thought you were just impressing them.

DON'T WASTE YOUR TIME ON HIM

Once in awhile in this business, you will encounter a real "bozo," who shows great intentions toward buying something from you or maybe selling something to you. Then they get real "flaky" and might tell you to call them back next week. You call back and they tell you to call the next week. This goes on for weeks and months, and can even go on indefinitely. You get excited at first then lose hope, then go up and down like a yo-yo. It drives you crazy. Face it: They are wasting your time. They either don't have the money or wish they did or, if they were trying to sell something to you, they just can't seem to part with the item. They might not have the social skills to explain their intentions, but scratch them off your list so you can pursue the next deal without the worry of them hanging out there.

This is different than the honest person who does take months and more to get the collection to sell to you, or who is trying to put together the cash to buy from you. You need to have some insight and determine between the two types and realize whom you can work with. The "weird" ones get obvious after a short while.

Realize that there is always a good deal just around the corner, and most likely better product to buy than you could possibly afford. Remember, if you are selling, there is always a good buyer available for quality product, so move on.

BE CAREFUL WHO YOU TRUST

When I started out in a certain area of picking books, I had an opportunity to buy a full set of Zane Grey books that still had their dust jackets on and were in "unread" condition. They were bought many years ago and set on a bookshelf. I really wasn't into Zane Gray, nor did I have any idea of the books' popularity. I knew someone who would know, though—an old-timer I met at several book fairs and whose expertise I felt comfortable with. Jake was a major Western Americana collector, so told him about the deal and how the person said he'd sell them to me for $3 apiece. Jake told me that's about all they were worth, at least that's what he'd pay for them, or maybe a little more.

I put off buying them, as I saw no profit in the deal and figured that I'd be better served putting my dollars in stuff I had interest in. Years later, and after I'd gained more experience, I saw several of the same editions in worse shape sitting on a shelf in a bookstore between ten and fifteen times that offered price. The opportunity to buy them had long since gone. Old Jake I guess was just trying to get a good deal, too. This, folks, is how you get smarter.

SELL ONLY TO PEOPLE WHO HAVE THE CASH

One major problem with your local market is buddies. You might get into loads of good stuff and have friends and acquaintances with similar interests. You can easily overload the local market and they can easily run out of cash. You might then find yourself running a tab on these folks and pretty quickly, you can find you have a list of people each owing you several hundred dollars.

Trust and friendship are just a part of the situation. Yes, you might find a few go south on you, and you lose the stuff, the money, and the friendship. But then your cash flow gets strangled, and when you are short of cash, you can't buy the good deals that come your way. This is discouraging and dangerous—dangerous, in that you are tempted to go into debt yourself to buy the deal that comes your way. The first problem is you borrow the cash (dependent on the cash your friend owes you). Then you may only get the cash from the friend in little amounts that you then spend away.

So you borrowed the money (because someone owes you that much) and buy some new items, and the person finally pays you back. But you spend that money he pays you back on a new deal that comes along, rather than paying the debt. (Yikes!)

So remember these things when dealing with your local market; don't pile it on your friends. Don't give credit. Trade, swap, or barter if you need to. Sell to the folks who have the cash. Experiment outside of your area to find new customers. They will probably pay you higher prices, too.

FORGIVE THE DEBT

I had a situation where I let a person take some surplus electronic scrap that was loaded with gold-plated devices. He was to salvage the gold and take a percentage, giving me a healthy profit. After he took the scrap, we spoke several times. He had a few delays, due to health problems, and so I waited. Later on, he and I would talk and he'd keep assuring me all was going well. His delays kept happening and eventually I got the hint: he ripped me off.

This made me more upset. I called daily for weeks. He wouldn't return the call, so I'd leave angry messages. Then I finally figured out that I would never resolve it and get satisfaction. He was dishonest—I was the victim.

My mind needs some type of closure to things like this. I called one day and spoke to one of his children. The message went something like this, "I had some product your father was going to process for me. It had a value of several hundred dollars. I have been calling for weeks and weeks, you know that because you took some of the messages. I know he is not going to pay me or return the stuff. I know he's being dishonest with me. But please tell him for me that I forgive the debt. This will be my last phone call, thank you."

It really helped. I could scratch his name and number off my list. I don't have to be upset anymore. I learned some marvelous lessons. It was a valuable experience. Besides, there was no longer a victim.

WATCH OUT FOR PEOPLE WHO DON'T UNDERSTAND WHAT PICKING IS ABOUT

I was in a thrift store awhile back, talking to a full-time professional picker I know. We were talking about some of his finds and methods. A woman who overheard our conversation immediately got angry with him and started spouting off on how he was a real creep. After all, he was there "stealing" all the good buys first and then taking his finds out to the swap meet and tripling his money. I was expecting to see her start swinging her purse. He tried to defend himself by explaining how it's his job and living to do this. She wouldn't hear of it. Didn't she realize that the thrift store she respected so much was doing the same thing? They are a non-profit organization that depends on items given to them … for free, and then they price it, and sell it to the public. I'll bet you she has found a good deal more than once and profited from it.

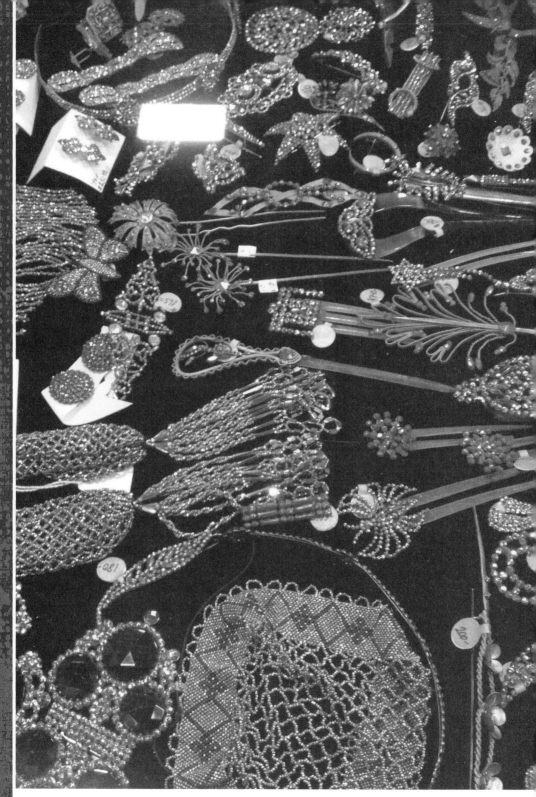

Whether it's rhinestone jewelry like above or some other antique or collectible, you'll do much better as a picker if you have a specialty.

Chapter 2

....

The Philosophy of Picking

FEAST OR FAMINE SYNDROME

I call it a syndrome. It happens to the best of us, but if you are careful and recognize that it's happening, you might be better off. I've had days where it's been very slim pickings and all I see is junk. The problem is, I buy some of that junk I wouldn't normally because I'm not finding anything and feel I just have to buy something. I've also had days and opportunities where there is so much stuff, it's overwhelming and I usually end up passing on many items I'd normally buy in a minute on a slow day. Feast and famine. At one end of the spectrum, you are wasting money, and at the other end, you don't have enough money to buy all you want.

I think many of us need to be more selective and careful when there is famine to not piddle away all those needed dollars. It really adds up. If you can turn the dollars fast selling all the small stuff quickly, then it's okay.

Some pickers have excellent cash control. Their inventory turns regularly, and they have promptly paying customers. They keep their cash flow in order and have the dollars when they are needed to invest in opportunities. Many pickers, however, seem to work "hand-to-mouth" and never have the cash to buy the good stuff when it's available. They use credit too much or they dabble in the small stuff because the high-end products are out of their league.

Several just plain don't know how or where to sell their goods. Many people also try to keep too much stuff, rather than moving it on. They also make many bad buying decisions.

When beginning in a new area of collectibles, especially, you may need to be much more selective than you want to be, but go for the known and sought after items and select the best quality pieces.

Working hand-to-mouth at first has some side benefits, including getting creative. For example, you might pull some real good stunts in order to get something that you want. You might also be able to obtain cash almost magically to help you buy something you really want. Other amazing feats include deals such as "three-way trades" to various collectors and dealers. You might also have brilliant inspiration of what to sell or whom to sell to, when you are in a more needful situation. Experiences can become techniques to use later on, even when money isn't so tight. You can learn a great deal from the feast or famine syndrome.

On the days you will find more stuff than you can feasibly carry, and possibly pay for, have room for, or have time to go through, some options are to broker some of it; partner with someone for some of it; high-grade some of the better pieces and walk away from the rest; and if you get it all, quickly wholesale some of it. To prepare for days like this, it is always good to have the knowledge of values and potential customers, etc., because you have more choices.

PREACHING ABOUT WANTS

You'll have to bear with me while I do a bit of preaching. This is a product of my own understanding and rationalizing, but it is good information to help you know your seller and your customers as you start dealing. This whole business is based upon wants. You want, they want, we see, we like, we get, we show. Somehow we gather comfort from these worldly finite items, but it's all just stuff. It's plastic, glass, metal, paint, and color. It's inanimate, blind, and soulless. The worth of an item is only created by talking about it. Value is only a perception. Price is an absolute illusion. It is pride of ownership that drives people to collect. It's having something more or before the other guy that gives us victory. We somehow feel more valuable by having it.

The drive, the passion, and the obsession—all of the other stuff, whether historical, nostalgic, artful, important, or rare is only a rationalization. Compare your understanding of the topic above to the topic below. If you understand the above better, you will make it work better. You may be making a full-time living owning a successful business, or just supplementing an income. You might just do this for fun, or to satisfy a need to collect. On the other hand, if you get too hung up on the things, it will be difficult to sell or trade. You need to let go in order to make a profit.

If you let go, if you sell, you will move and turn over your inventory. You will have and find numerous more contacts and better items. You will grow. Hoarding ultimately hurts you. If, however, you sell to others who hoard, it serves to fulfill their needs and insatiable wants while it helps you. The more you give, the more you get.

ENTHUSIASM

Enthusiasm in anything is an asset. Enthusiasm also goes in surges and stages. You are on a hot trail. You just found out that a whole garage full of goodies is available. You just might have a chance to buy the entire lot at a good price. Better than that, no one else even knows it's for sale. This first stage is euphoria. You may dream about it, that is, if you can sleep! You count your shekels; you try to figure the profit you will realize if it goes through as you plan. You worry it might not happen. You worry about the competition finding out and out bidding you. You worry the seller will change their mind. You get "feelings" such as butterflies, sick pangs, and irritability.

The next stage is more controlled. Guess what, it is going to happen. The appointment is established, and the dollars are discussed. Transportation and storage is arranged. It's yours. The deal is done. The last stage is the possession, the victory. The euphoria and other physically felt emotions are gone. It's a controlled joy, or satisfaction. The stories can now be told. The travel, and the quest of obtaining it, are always more exciting than having the item. First comes the excitement, which helps you have the energy to obtain an item, then the reward.

SPECIALIZE AND LEARN

The best way to approach this business is to have a specialty—to know about certain items inside and out. There are a couple of ways to approach this. You may have already found a hobby that has kept your interest over many years. This is the best experience you can have. You already know what items cost and where to obtain them. As you look for products, your eyes and mind will be drawn to them before anyone else. I am always pleasantly surprised when I am going through an estate sale and have even arrived late and found items in my specialty in abundance. Everyone else passed them by. This is because I know something they don't know. It's because I've been interested

Many collectors have a specific niche they focus on, such as sewing machines. These were for sale at the San Jose, CA, flea market.

for so long, and have probably had experience selling or buying these items before.

This works for estate sales, yard sales, and local classified ads and even eBay. I actually enjoy picking products from eBay listings. Sometimes you can find some real jewels that everyone else misses. You can easily take better photos, describe better, test it out, and make a better title, or put it in a different category and double or triple your investment.

The other way is to learn and be curious. Watch other pickers and see what they are finding. If you get a chance to determine models or types, or names of products they are grabbing, make notes, and when you have time, research it on Google and eBay. You can also ask the other pickers questions. Many people love telling you about their killer finds. They like to boast about how much they made, and even share secrets, not realizing they are training their competition.

Sometimes I find this information from them, or watch what they buy, and when I search for it on eBay a few days later, or "save the search" by topic name and by my locality, sure enough, the actual item from my local picker friend shows up. This is a great way to find out more. You can see how much profit they made, especially if you remember how much they paid. If you continue to follow their listings, you'll find out lots of things, including what they like, how much they find, stuff you weren't aware of, and can even discover new sources for products as you follow their hints. All of this is information to help you specialize and KNOW more the next time. This information is free, but it just cost you some time. I have dozens of people I follow on eBay who are my competition. They don't know I'm looking and learning; eBay makes it automatic for me as I save the search, so when new items get posted, I am notified in an email.

REDISTRIBUTE THE WEALTH

I went to an open house at a large church-operated thrift store a couple of years ago and heard a talk by an individual who was employed there as a trainer. The thrift store not only sells stuff to help feed the poor, it has other functions. Besides a church welfare operation, individuals are trained to work in a variety of operations. The store purposely turns over a large population of employees, providing the community with a group of trained, capable workers, who would normally be unemployable people. They provide the donations to the public at low prices, or bargains, realizing many people cannot afford to buy at retail and need these products for their own use. They are well aware of the pickers and they refer to them as dealers. They understand that their store not only provides work and training for the individuals they employ, but provides a living to many others who sell the products found there. They consider their role is also to re-distribute the wealth. Seems like a worthy goal.

STEWARDSHIP

What do you have? Do you really own it? Ownership, better described as stewardship, is how all this stuff we are doing works. If you want to be good in this business, you need to understand how stewardship works. Very simply, someone makes something (or finds it in the earth), holds onto it for a while, uses it, keeps it, sells it, or gives it away. They have it for a while then someone else gets it. I hate to remind you, but you are temporary. This stuff you have is temporarily yours. Absolute ownership of physical items is impossible. Humans like to put big fancy comforting terms or descriptions of ways to keep it, like estate, foundation, trust, or bequeath, etc. Somehow we think this keeps our name with the item forever, but it really doesn't.

Have you ever seen a gold coin that was made in ancient Rome? Do you know the name of the original owner? Do you have any idea at all about who the owner was one generation ago? How about all those other generations? This coin's owners don't survive as long as the coin does. Ownership is a poor term. Stewardship is more accurate, but stewardship also carries with it another component—responsibility.

We are stewards of things right now. The previous owners are forgotten, and all the subsequent owners are unknown. This is why we fix and protect stuff that is especially historical. It's not in just having the thing or its dollar value. It's not just the rarity or only about pride. It's about respect.

When you deal with historical, vintage, classic, and important valuable items, you are a temporary custodian. You do have some responsibility. Examples include:

PROTECTION: You should have the proper storage area to keep any further damage from the elements, etc. You need to keep it safe from improper use, which includes poor restoration and cleaning (i.e. the damage caused by some antiques dealers' favorite tool, the wire brush … ouch!). Is it insured while in your possession?

IDENTIFICATION: What if you found a one-of-a-kind or an important prototype? This is not only valuable monetarily, but valuable historically.

DESTINATION: Does the important stuff go to museums or well-protected private collections? Do you deal with knowledgeable dealers?

You may have a variety of reasons for harvesting this stuff, just do it well! Discover it, collect it, identify it, appreciate it, enjoy it, and profit from it!

COLLECTING NICHES

It seems that the weirdest and most narrow fields of interest can yield the best and most interesting collections. My wife started years ago collecting snowmen and any time I found a vintage, ugly looking, or weird little snowman, I'd grab it for her. I was her snowman picker. Now every Christmas, she has an amazing snowman tree full of unique and some old and classic pieces. It has grown beyond the tree to an entire bookcase and the tree full of snow people. It is a pleasure to look at. We have grandkids who marvel at the scenes.

I collect old radios and some old radio "niches" i.e. I collect tubes, and early radio advertising and radio parts advertising items. Do you see how you can become more and more specialized into tiny little branches within your main field? The finer the niche, the more unique, interesting, and valuable your collection can be.

To connect with other collectors and help one another achieve success in the world of antiques and collectibles, whether it is as a hobby, for profit, or both, consider starting a group in your area and having meetings to share ideas and talk shop, give appraisals, and even buy or sell each other's items. You could also attend swaps meets, estate sales, or auctions together.

KISSING TOADS

Another dealer I met once said, "You need to kiss an awful lot of toads to be able to find a prince." He used this as slogan when picking. You have to visit many sales in order to find one or two good items. This also goes for new products, leads, and stories. Just being active in this, you will find out many things by people bragging, or conversing. If you advertise, even with a simple business card, you will get leads. It could be as simple as "I Buy X" and your name and cell phone number. Tell friends what you collect or buy. One day your prince or princess will come.

Holiday-themed items are popular with some collectors.

A booth at an antiques show with various figurines. I recognize Whimpey and Popeye. My parents would recognize the others; my kids and grandkids - none.

Chapter 3

....

Stories
From the Field

I n the picking business, it's a good idea to try and find a picker pro who doesn't mind sharing some of his or her knowledge and experience, and then after you have gained more experience, you should help another newcomer.

When I started out, my now-good friend Mike was an elusive legend and my big competition. He seemed to get everywhere first. If I was looking for something or answering an ad, Mike had already been there and found the prize.

I attended an auction seeking a certain item advertised in the classifieds. When the lot I wanted came up, I made a bid... then Mike upped it. We went higher and higher until I finally got it. As I went to pay for it, Mike came over to see who the other person was who was bidding against him. He turned out to be a pleasant guy and I learned lots of good information from him. We became friends and bought and sold to each other.

Mike did real well for himself when he was a picker. He had a flexible work schedule, which helped him to get out anytime to find the good stuff and he did find the good stuff. He was also honest in his dealings with all the folks selling him stuff, and when he sold and made his profit, all of them went to helping his family.

He was always reporting how he bought things at low prices and sold them for surprisingly larger ones. For example, he found some antique country furniture cupboards he paid $15 a piece for and sold a couple of hours later for $375 each.

He taught me how he looked in the paper and online at all of the ads, marked the best possibilities, and then looked online in a reverse directory. Then he phoned the people before a sale started to ask questions and save himself from lots of time driving around. It also helped him prioritize his list so he got there first. One good tip he discovered is that the city directory, in the library, sometimes lists how long the phone number was assigned to an individual, which helped him determine how old the stuff might be in the house; if it shows the residence has been there for forty years, there is an excellent possibility for good antiques.

He also taught me how you can usually find things at yard and garage sales that aren't for sale—at least they weren't for sale before you came by. He always asked people if they had any old furniture and other things on his list. He usually found the best stuff this way. Other pickers and dealers can't understand how he could find so many good items, but he was essentially going out to ask people door-to-door if they had any antiques for sale. This isn't done much now, but he did find a yard sale an open invitation to ask.

A financial difficulty forced Mike to stop collecting years ago and give up his extensive collection. After that, he determined he would never get that close to things again. He considered himself a mercenary, only in it for the money.

I've seen many other pickers who are mercenaries and they always seem to work hand to mouth. They usually sell a find quickly and take a shorter profit just to take the quick doubling of their money. They feel pretty clever and satisfied with this, which is okay, I guess, but rarely do I see any reinvesting or searching and waiting for the best realization of profit.

I have found many times that as I wait—especially on the good items—I learn more about the market. I learn that the value in the price guide is low for a certain item or I buy an item and months later see it in an antiques magazine article. I need to let it age a bit sometimes, especially for the good stuff.

I know another full-time picker who does things completely different and dropped out of the system because he was tired of working for others. Frank stops ten to twelve times each day picking for goods and makes enough to support himself and get a few things he likes. He goes after practical stuff, as he feels there is good money to be made in these items. His interest personally isn't in antiques, as there is too much competition, but the 1950s are interesting to him. There has been a recent craze for '50s period looks and he says he has been pretty successful in finding and selling many such items.

Frank warns how easy it is to find good deals and over buy. You have to remember you don't usually turn items over immediately and if you sit on the goods too long, you can get into a lot of trouble. He also warns of the horrible dishonesty that is in this business and absolutely hates to see the mark-up that a dealer makes after he sells to them. This is what drives him toward wanting his own store.

After thinking over what Frank told me, I discovered something: The dealer has to buy an item at a good price so he can make his profit. Let's say he has to buy an item for $70 and try and sell it for $100 (Frank doesn't like to see that $100 price tag). But realize that the dealer was not able to buy it for $10 like Frank did. Who gives up more? Let's break it down here:

"Fifties" chair bought at a thrift store: **$10**
Retail value: **$100**
Dealer cost: **$70**
Thrift store: makes **$10**, gives up **$90**
Picker: makes **$60**, gives up **$40**
Dealer: makes **$30**, gives up **$70**

Now, this isn't always the spread; sometimes a savvy dealer makes a large profit margin because he has a customer or can sit on the inventory for a while. Or he just has a better feel for the worth of the item than the picker. But the rest of the equation is that the customer paid $100 for it. (He really pays.)

OFF-THE-STREET NETWORKING

My best deals have always been "off-the-street" deals. In the sales profession, "taking it off the street" means to identify a potential big sale for a customer and sell it to him before the competition ever has a chance to hear about it. The buy never goes out for bid. It is literally taken off the street.

This also works on buying material before your dealer friends ever hear about it. If you are searching the same places all the other pickers are searching, the only thing you have on your side is timing.

To get an opportunity to take it off the street, you need to network: let other folks know what you look for. They say or hear things, and it opens your exposure to many other opportunities to find what you are looking for. Don't be shy about what you are looking for, either. You can just tell them you "collect" you don't need to say you pick or deal in the items. If you have a specialty, let others know about it. Show off your best pieces. Keep things on your desk. Tell friends and relatives what you do. They probably toss out or give away these things all the time.

PICKERS TEAM UP

Yep, a picker can have a picker find items for the first picker. I, being a picker and collector and somewhat a dealer, have a few other pickers call me with their finds. They pick for me and I pick for some of them. It works out pretty well. The best arrangement is if your other picker would have never normally picked, nor is interested in picking what you go after. Otherwise they might sell to you at much higher prices, or be in direct competition. The best pickers are good friends or relatives, or someone you can trust. Those folks who understand your obsession will do you a good favor once in awhile. The more you buy from other pickers, the more often you will get calls to see the stuff first. After all, they want to profit as quickly as they can on their finds, too.

I have an agreement with a good friend, who has different interests than mine: I find a few early paperback novels and some certain glassware items he goes for, and in turn, he finds me old radios.

You really have to know about the stuff a picker is interested in, though. For example, I was going to pick early mining lamps for a dealer and he assured me he saw radios in various digs he went to. It happened that he brought me a bunch of old radios, but they were just a bunch of junkers a few years old and not worth a dime apiece. It was hard to tell him the truth, after he invested his good money, although, I kind of think he made his money back when I sold him some mining lamps I picked for him.

I love these old pharmacy specimen jars, but sometimes they are full of poison!

When you're traveling, it's worth it to stop at any thrift stores, pawn shops, estate sales, and antiques shows that may be in the towns you're passing through.

DEALING WITH COMPETITORS

You will find lots of competition in this business and as you identify who these other pickers are, you have an edge.

AGGRESSIVE COMPETITION: These are the people who can be the most troublesome. They go after the same things you do. They know prices. They know the hot spots. They know all the buyers and sellers for the same things. These people can also be your supplier and you might even buy from them. They may also be your customers! (Strange circles, huh?) The aggressive competition could also be friends one day, and folks that would scoop you in a minute the next.

PASSIVE COMPETITION: They are people who might not even collect the items you look for; they just happen to find an item and buy it. You might be going crazy trying to find a specific item and they haul it out to their car smiling. But if there is someone else after the same item you are, that means there is demand and this helps the value of things.

PICKING VACATIONS AND TRIPS

When I travel, I like to visit all the different collectors, dealers, and places I can to broaden my vision and find not only stuff, but information, too. I like to ask questions of the pros, those who seem to be the best in their field or at least have good success. Ask if they will let you record your conversation, or videotape or photograph their collection. You can learn an awful lot by doing this. At the very least, you need to write down in your notes what went on, any model numbers and prices gathered, and ideas you got after your visit.

I also love to trade when I'm on the road. You see different stuff in different areas, and what might be common in one part of the country might be scarce somewhere else. So take a box of stuff, if you have room, for trading and selling, and also have cash with you because you may find good deals.

On your trip, figure out what some likely stops will be by looking in the Yellow Pages for antiques dealers, auctioneers, collectibles, estates, pawnbrokers, second-hand stores, surplus and salvage merchandise, swap meets, and thrift stores. Call a few places or people and ask questions about who the active collectors are and where the locals find certain items. Ask about clubs, museums, or special collections. It is truly amazing to see how much information you get by a few simple questions. Once you get started, you can really network quite deeply and find some super contacts. If you travel with some "trading stock," it really opens up doors, too.

I have several times contacted people who actually pick me up from my hotel, drive me across town to their home to see their collection, and let me purchase or trade items from their collections. You can find all sorts of treasures this way.

I also keep a directory of names that I gather from ads from everywhere "just in case" I ever travel to these particular cities. As I read an interesting classified ad, dealers ad, or brochure, I put it in the directory. When I am fortunate to travel to that city, I have lots of people to phone, visit, or trade with. I always keep a journal of my contacts and visits, too. When you use social media, like Facebook, LinkedIn, and Google+, you can build an amazing resources list you can use to contact people when traveling.

YOU SNOOZE, YOU LOSE

Here's one of those experiences where you can learn from my mistakes. I received a call from a fellow picker friend of mine about a "great score" he came across: an entire collection of more than 200 antique radios. As he started to describe the pieces, I got excited, but when he told me where he got them, my heart sank. I could have easily had the opportunity, if I'd been more astute. Weeks before, I found an old jukebox at a thrift store that I thought I could turn for a quick profit, and so my first call was to a collector. Somewhere in the back of my mind I knew he had radios, but I wasn't thinking about radios at that moment; I just wanted to move the jukebox. But he wasn't interested because he was trying to get out of the business. Now here's where I should have asked if he was also going to get rid of the radios, but I didn't and missed my cue.

The way I do things, however, is I try and make lemonade out of lemons, so what did I do? I went over and hi-graded some of those radios from my friend and I actually got some pretty good deals.

CAUTIONARY TALE

When you find a deal on an item and want to sell it, you need to proceed slowly and study the market, as a friend of mine learned.

He was visiting an antiques showcase mall where he has a case of products for sale and the shop owner told him about someone who wanted to sell an old phonograph. After much delay, my friend followed up on the referral and went to look at it. It was much more than an old phonograph and like nothing he had ever seen before; it was a large Chippendale-style, inlaid wood on burled walnut cabinet, filled with a giant mechanism. This unit might even have been one-of-a-kind. My friend put off buying it, though, because he wasn't sure if he could move it. The seller finally talked him into taking it for $100.

The cabinet was manufactured in Salt Lake City in the 1920s and in wonderful shape and well taken care of for many years. Someone had removed all of the tubes, but otherwise, it looked fairly intact. The "Ordomatic" had a lower cabinet that included a radio and the most amazing phonograph contraption. It had a four-sided turntable that would rotate after each record was played. It would take a record that was stacked vertically on one side, and feed it into the side turntable; that record was then fed into the vertical turntable by a rotating coil the set of records was stacked in. Once the record on top was finished playing, the tone arm would lift and the entire turntable would rotate, bringing the new selection to the top. The last record that played would "pay off" into the coil on the other side, and get stacked with the others.

Was this a radio? Was it a phonograph? Could it have been one of the earliest attempts at a jukebox or was it pre-juke box?

My friend did minimal research and found a fellow out of state that advertised for similar items. This potential buyer asked the price and my friend pulled a number out of the air and confidently blurted out $3,000. Now, the first hint that this price was too low is that the dealer was not fazed with this seemingly large amount. He said to send some photographs and he'd send a moving company to collect the item and bring it to him.

After hearing this story, I challenged my friend's attempt to sell this important item so soon. First of all, he only had $100 invested and didn't even know what the thing was. I told him he probably needed to speak to some people in the associated markets, like jukebox or phonograph collectors, not just radio people, and take the time to identify it and research the market. That way he wouldn't be leaving a lot of money on the table and enjoy some more profit on the item.

Now, usually, those who try and squeeze every penny out of their finds suffer somewhat. Part of the problem is that you may gain a bad reputation of not being fair to deal with. You also need to realize that it takes much more time to study and sell every item you get for top dollar. This is disastrous to your cash flow.

In the case of single, one-time important discoveries, however, you need to move slowly. You'll need to find out more information, and find the right buyer at the right price. The temptation to make that $2,900 profit is pretty great, but what if you were able to make twice or more if you just added a few hours research and a few good phone calls? Maybe a well-written and well-placed advertisement would do it. It would take many more hours and much more work and effort to make that much on your money doing lots of $10 or even $100 deals. Don't be too quick to make a buck on the important stuff. If it's a big deal, make a big deal out of it!

A chair made of recycled hockey sticks is perfect for a game room.

HE HAS A REPUTATION TO KEEP

I was speaking with a dealer who has a large sales space at our local swap meet. He brought up a point that I feel is good to cover. He mentioned a local picker we both know well. He sells just about everything he gets and has learned how turn over is important. He makes a profit on everything he sells, but has a reputation for selling "cheap." What happens is that once you buy from him and get a good deal, you feel you are entitled to always get a good deal from him. He couldn't get list price on anything from people who buy from him regularly. You want to move as much product as you can and be well known. You don't mind wholesaling, but you want to make a good profit on the big stuff, too.

How can you do both?

You are more anonymous if you sell some items in an antiques showcase mall. You might try moving the rare and expensive items out of state. Be patient on the important and expensive pieces—if they want it, they'll pay. Try running an ad in the online or newspaper classifieds; you'll meet new people.

YOU WIN SOME AND LOSE SOME

Here's another story to learn from. You get a call from a fellow picker. He has a couple of items in your field of interest that are new and currently sell for $300 apiece. He wants to sell them to you for $150 each. You hem and haw, saying you'll check around to see if you can flip them, so you call your contacts or anyone who comes to mind and find limited interest.

You call back less excited because you don't have an immediate sale for the items, but know they do have value. So now you offer a much lower price of $50 each because you think you might be able to move them one of these days. He says he'll see what he might do elsewhere.

The next day calls come back from your previous inquiries. Someone told someone else who now really wants one. You could have made a good profit, had you known. You call your supplier back, but they already sold for $75 each. Gosh, you'd have paid that much. Could have, should have, would have … you know the rest.

Guess what you just did? You just paid for tuition. Yes, just exactly like if you were going to college. It is tuition in the field you are pursuing. It's tuition in the art of negotiations. This is how you learn the business. You learn prices, what is a good deal, when is a good deal, etc. Congratulations, you're in the thick of it.

Ed Uditis of Florida has some fun in his booth at the 2013 Brimfield Antiques Show.

Chapter 4

....

Hot Spots

The following places and haunts are prime spots for picking choice antiques, collectibles, and other items, whether you are looking to buy or sell.

ANTIQUES SHOWS

You may be one of the fortunate people to live nearby a major outdoor antiques show like the Brimfield Antiques Show in Brimfield, Massachusetts, or another ginormous mega show. Attending a major show like this is a big event and most large cities have nice local and regional antiques shows. One way to easily find out is to visit any local antiques store in your area and gather the many fliers usually left by the entrance. Ask the dealers about the shows listed, and if they go to them as sellers or buyers. If you go to a show as a picker or buyer, you will need to be highly selective, as most of the inventory has been thoroughly researched online to determine the value. Plus, be aware that the price is probably higher because they know that people will haggle and they will need to lower the price. The price will end up being the market value likely. If you go to one of these shows, it will be a good opportunity to sell the items you are picking during the months before. One benefit is the show removes all of the pain and preparation required by selling on eBay. You do not need to photograph, describe, test, package, ship, deal with bad buyers, handle returns, pay eBay, pay PayPal, etc., but you do need to organize, display, haul weight, clean, price stickers, and deal with the retail public. Things you need to deal with are tables, receipts, local taxes, theft, damage, credit card processing (use PayPal here, or Square with your smart phone). Plus, you will need to take a high percentage back home when you are finished, presumably to sell on eBay eventually.

The Brimfield Antiques Show

I'd like to give some thoughts on my visit to the Brimfield Antiques Show in Massachusetts: It was a blast! This trip was actually the second visit to Brimfield; my first was many years ago. I was a casual collector then and it was overwhelming to see the activity there. The second time I went with a real purpose. I was ready and had certain areas and dealers I wished to visit. It was fun and interesting, but tiring. There are thousands of dealers spread over a large expanse and I was there only two days, but by the end of the second day, I had "antique presentation overload." You can only see and process so much information. Because of the sensory bandwidth limitation, I found the best way to approach it was to slow down a little bit and talk to people. I found that there are distinct types of people there:

1. **ANTIQUES DEALER COMPANIES.** They are organized, have well-working nice fixtures and layouts, and their booth is clean and orderly. They have high antiques store prices. They have done this for many years, and have probably built up a clientele. I am sure they bring things for certain prize customers that no one will even see otherwise.

2. **PICKERS.** This is what they do for a living: go out for months and pick and find interesting things to try and sell. Much of what they have is based on what they know about and have had success with before. They clean out estates and go to auctions, and bring what they can to the show.

3. **COLLECTORS.** These are collectors that have found that they can clean out much of their collection here, so they can go buy that great item that they need for that collection. This show is a way for them to upgrade their seconds, duplicates, and culls.

4. **SPECIALIZED SALES.** Here you will find a dealer or picker who has had a recent find they wish to sell. Because of their reputation and contacts, they found a special lot. They were contacted to buy a specific collection; or, they fell into a large cache of something. They go there to unload what

I walked up to Harry Hepburn at Brimfield. He was telling someone he "cut his teeth on tools." I asked him if his teeth ever got better…

Put your sign out and you will get great new contacts for buyers and sellers.

they can, and to have Brimfield be an avenue for future sales of the collection. They use Brimfield as an advertising medium. These can be the most interesting dealers there. They have stuff that has been in private museums for years, and now is available again.

5. **BUYERS.** I think there are many dealers there with stuff for sale, but looking for contacts for buying their type of product interest. Many hang a sign noting their wants and have brochures, etc.

6. **FLEA MERCHANTS.** I am sorry, but many booths I saw were from people hoping to collect a few bucks on what looked like it had been dragged to hundreds of sales, had been rained on many times, and was just yard sale junk. They probably do make money somehow, but there is no theme or organization whatsoever. They dump junk out on a table, and scrape it back into the boxes when they leave, ready for the next show.

7. **VENDORS.** These are the large booths of newly made antique-looking collectibles made in China or Mexico mostly sold to decorators. These vendors are not trying to sell counterfeit or reproduction knock offs; they are just selling new décor.

Going to a large show like Brimfield is like attending a pickers' convention. There are pickers buying and selling and learning and teaching, just like any other professional convention. It is endless networking and you hear stories and techniques. It's actually a whole lot more fun than a regular business trade show.

You should bring plenty of business cards and try to collect ones from all of your good contacts—make sure you write on the card something about the person or product that was interesting. If they do not have a card, ask for their information and write it on the back of one of your own cards. Tell people what you are looking for and find out what their "specialty" is. Ask people what their wants are. Start a want list and contact list. You'll be surprised how friendly people are, and how much you can learn. Astute dealers will keep you on their picker's list, and contact you and even bring stuff for you at the next show.

The biggest problem you will have is traffic. If you are planning on getting to a show opening at 9 a.m., be careful: You have the drive time there, and everybody else is driving there on a small single-lane road. (Add a half hour if it's busy). Then you need to park. It will cost money, and the closest lots will fill up first. Then you need to get in line. The show will cost something, too. All I am suggesting is that you plan and leave plenty of time if you wish to be an early buyer.

You really need good shoes, since you will be walking for miles. You will also need to bring an umbrella and/or a rain poncho—when it rains, it can be torrential there.

If you are only there to buy cheap and sell high, you actually can be successful. I have heard stories of dealers in the show, who have their own tables, buying an item and then selling it later at the same show and making a killing. If you have a space, and are selling, people will come up with things to sell you based on your specialty, and they very well may have bought it from another dealer at the show. This is a picker selling to pickers in a perfect economy.

You can see how, with experience and opportunity, you can buy and sell up repeatedly for the entire week. Trading is also included in this mix of transactions. To turn over your increased dollars, you need to be creative and work it well, but it's possible. If you are determined and smart, you could walk in with a few dollars and leave at the end of the show with hundreds or much higher.

Other Brimfield Tips

T-SHIRTS. I wore a T-shirt that said I collect old radios and tubes. I had people walk up to me and hand me cards and brochures. They would describe

Did you come close to guessing the price of this Enigma cipher machine from P. 5?

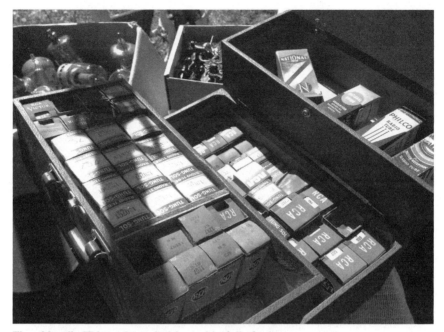

The old radio/TV repairman's tube caddy, full of tubes.

what they saw over on the next aisle of dealers. They asked me for advice on items they had for sale. They promised to contact me when they cleaned out an estate next time, admitting they didn't know what to do with the last lot they had.

BUSINESS CARDS. My business card has a long list of things I buy and sell. This opened up many more doors and much conversation. One lady in a dealer booth had a whole bunch of old empty radio tube caddies. I asked where all the tubes were. She said she passed on them because she didn't know anything about them. I had a great time drawing a short "picker's guide" for electron tubes. I drew an outline shape of the oldest and most valuable types of tubes with a few part numbers and what to look for, and which ones to pass on, and what to pay. She was so grateful. It was fun and she will call me when she comes across tubes in the future.

One thing I would do was hand dealers my card and say, "Here's my card, in-case you ever come across any of the things listed and want to call me." I could tell this is not done much because of the responses I received. If I was a dealer at a show like Brimfield, I'd collect cards in a bowl, have a want list

It's a helpful and fun idea to wear T-shirts at Brimfield, or any show, that advertises what you collect.

sign-up card, and maybe have a prize to give away. I'm pretty sure we would be surprised at who some of these people are walking around, and how much they are spending. I was at one booth where a buyer had just purchased a vintage corkscrew for $550. I was dumbfounded. I asked the dealer, *"$550?"* He told me that earlier he sold one for over $5,000! Corkscrews? He said you need to look for corkscrews with some sort of special advertising or ones that "do crazy things in order to operate." This is the type of instruction you receive all day long at a big show like Brimfield. You need to move around and ask questions and talk to people. Network, make friends, and contacts.

NEGOTIATING. I never did pay full price for anything I bought there. In one instance, I honestly had forgotten to go to an ATM and get cash. As I looked in my wallet, explaining how I needed to go get cash, the dealer said what I had was fine and so I bought his item. I used the lack of cash as my negotiating tool here.

Old pattern molds from a foundry make fantastic wall hangings. These molds were originally pressed into sand then the cavity created had molten metal poured into it for a precision casting. This dealer had tens of thousands of these.

Rare telegraph keys and sounders.

Tonja and Brad Harler visited Brimfield from Pennsylvania. We talked about her tube caddy and radio tubes.

In two other instances, I showed interest in an item with two different dealers. I kept a mental note of where they were. (**Note**: either draw yourself a map or get one and mark it. I really had a difficult time remembering where I had parked my car for one of the days.) A couple of hours had passed and I went back; the items were still there. In both instances, I was able to negotiate down to about half the price. I used "time" as my biggest negotiating tool here. The dealers talked to me previously, knew I had an interest, and realized they had no other interest in all the time I was away. I was back with the cash and they agreed to the lower price. If sales are slow, and they need to have sales, the price drops. This also goes for your local estate sales. Go back the next day and offer a whole lot less. They need to move the stuff, and the last day is even better.

PORTERS. At Brimfield, they have many healthy strong young people with carts all over the place willing to haul your purchases to your vehicle, to the on-site UPS Store, or to your own booth. They charge by the job that depends on the size and weight. This is a great back-saving service.

PLANNING YOUR TRIP. There are many websites with much information on Brimfield, and there are all kinds of free pamphlets and magazines onsite. This will help you remember and plan your next visit. There is a great book I recommend on some adventures of dealing at Brimfield: *Killer Stuff and Tons of Money: An Insider's Look at the World of Flea Markets, Antiques, and Collecting* by Maureen Stanton.

I suppose that shows like this, as large as they are, would still be considered local or maybe regional. I was a little curious how people were always shocked when I mentioned I was from Utah. They could not imagine why I would come all that way. Yet, when I heard a lady who was visiting from France negotiating with a dealer, they did not seem so surprised. I suppose there are "French pickers," too.

My Booth at a Local Show

Last year I put together a booth for a local antiques show I have attended before. Now, usually I just sell my antiques online on eBay or to individual collectors or dealers, but I really wanted to try a booth.

Pre-show organization is important. I had the tables I needed but needed to find table covers and skirting, which I bought on eBay for a fourth of the price I could find locally. You need all the small office supplies including scissors, tape, stickers, pens, business cards, dollar bills and change, receipt books, etc. I needed to spend countless hours finding, cleaning, identifying, pricing, and boxing up the entire inventory to sell. I needed cases, shelves, and display units. I produced a few signs and placed a few good written ads in a local online classified that showed there was hundreds of views. Set up is a lot of work and I had three pick-up loads for a 10-foot x 10-foot booth. Once it was ready, I had to cover it with bed sheets.

On opening day, certain times were dead slow, while some were hectic. I talked to people who praised my inventory, some real know-it-all types, and even some people who, I'm sorry to say, were irritating and downright weird. The retail public is all kinds of people. They ask questions, they tell you what they have, and show you stuff. They start bragging and boasting about their items. They want free appraisals. There was an actual "crazy lady" who was in my booth. She walked and talked for at least 45 minutes about each item she saw. But then there are the true gems! I made some wonderful contacts and I had them write down their names, phone numbers, and email addresses. I also learned a lot about stuff and took notes from what some people taught me, which was valuable. I also did some trading, which I really enjoy.

There are certain pickers I know who came by my booth and I noticed a strange human behavior. One guy looked at everything in my booth and I know very well that if one of the items had been at an estate sale with the same price, he would have bought it. But this was an antiques show, so he didn't buy it. I've noticed myself doing the same thing. I know that when there is competition around, especially at a live auction, I pay more than what I saw priced at a sale or a show like this.

I was bemoaning the show to my wife, who was also an amazing help for me. I said the hours spent at the show and pre show, and post show all added up would have been better spent listing these items on eBay. Then I thought the stuff that doesn't sell is already to list. Plus I did make money at the show, and I made some amazing contacts. I started planning the next year's show, and how I might do things better.

Local shows are so limited in market. You can put out hundreds of items each person can see, but online, your buyers will see only one of your items usually, but there are thousands of eyes looking at that item. Sometimes you make enough on one of your sales that you can justify a purchase at one of the other booths. I did. But I started with, "I have a booth on the other side. Can you give a fellow dealer a discount?" Yep, got $20 off.

You need to constantly be straightening and moving stuff around, especially when something sells. I also did some "marking down" on prices to see if it helped. Then there is the State Sales Tax Men. They come around with a paper to figure your sales, and to give you the tax percentage amount to collect. The agents are there in one of the last hours of the day to collect. Keep good records.

A rare Charlie McCarthy radio that came with its original box.

I made friends with a couple of the dealers there. One is going to help me with glassware I find, and I will help him with antique tech stuff.

Price Sticker Ideas for Cases and Displays

When I priced items for the show, I made sure everything had a price sticker. Cheap stuff I priced to sell fast; bigger stuff I priced even higher than what I saw as completed items sell for on eBay. This was because I knew people would ask for a discount. I hate it when walking around a show like this, and seeing case after case of unpriced items dealers display. First of all, I hate asking the price on every little thing. Plus, I am looking for good deals and I want to see them fast; I don't want to have to stop and talk about them to someone with a sales pitch. PRICE YOUR ITEMS!

This is also a problem at antiques malls. I have many times walked through an antiques mall and saw a locked case and one or more items I had an interest in, but I didn't see the price. Dealers need to put a visible price on every item in the case. As a collector, and a picker, I usually just keep moving, never to return, because it is just too big of a pain to ring for the shopkeeper to bring a key. I also hate it when you can tell there is a price *sticker on the bottom of the piece*, but you can't see it. Books are usually the biggest problem, as the seller

It was nice to see prices on all of the items in this antiques show display. People hate to have to ask what the price is.

prices it in pencil on the inside front cover. Books should have a bookmark type of tag, plainly marked with the price out the top. Everything should have a visible price on it. In a large mall especially, people zoom through the store, only scanning the case. Here's the secret: You usually have one or two seconds to tell them about everything you are selling. Antiques pickers frequent these malls and book scouts, too, all moving fast when they are there.

Another of our secrets, and a way to add value to your items, and *a way to keep customers in front of your case* is to print a small card. Include historical information, descriptions, dates, etc. on the card, with a price. If you need to reduce the price, don't show it on sale with a cheaper marked down price. This is a way of telling the customer, "Something is wrong with the item, and I just found out about it, so now it's cheaper." Always print a new label.

I went to an estate sale put on by a savvy dealer, who did something I have never seen before. He attached a piece of blue painter's tape on each item, and put his white price sticker on the blue tape. First of all, every item is plainly marked and your eyes readily find the well-marked price. He personally is an antiques picker, dealer, and collector himself, and knows how important it is to protect the item with the painter's tape. It is easy to remove and will not mark or deface the finish or cover, etc.

ANTIQUES STORES AND MALLS

The traditional store is a company that is owned by an individual or people who own most of the inventory displayed. One of the nicest operations to happen is the showcase mall. These can be called malls even if they are smaller shops. These showcase malls have many display cases and booths that are filled with consigned inventory owned by small dealers, pickers, collectors, and others trying to move some products. Sometimes even other antiques stores put cases in other areas trying to get more exposure for their items.

This all makes an interesting display of product. The variety is diverse and anything goes: Antiques, collectibles, books, toys, and stuff of all kinds can be found. These stores almost create an historical museum of sorts since each dealer usually specializes in his or her own type of products, but the big difference between this and a museum is that this stuff is for sale. It's a great education to go through these stores learning about products and pricing. You'll be astounded at how many items you will see for sale that you passed up while out picking. Remember, however, just because it's for sale and has a healthy price on it doesn't mean anyone will ever buy it.

Here's how I work an antiques store:

I am usually pretty focused on what I search for and collect. I have many interests and areas of expertise. This list is narrow enough that I can sort those items from the many thousands found in a typical store. I quickly scan sections, shelves, and rooms and move on. This is particularly helpful when you are trying to see many stores. Some towns have concentrated antiques store shopping areas. To see much, you need to look quickly. Certain areas such as my collectibles or books slow me down. Many areas (even entire stores) I can quickly skip because I see they are not in my area. This is probably because I am just not informed or educated on the items.

I go in with the attitude that I'm going to learn something. I usually do and keep good notes of the visit. I also pick up any business cards, because new contacts are part of the learning I'm seeking. If the dealer has a certain expertise or specialty, it's noted on the card. The big opportunity is seeing how much things cost. It's also good to see how things are displayed and learn the merchandising techniques used to sell products. Make notes of displays that catch your eye.

I have picked up great deals even in the high-priced stores. You can even find thrift store prices occasionally, because of a less-informed dealer. If it's something I know well, and it's priced right (and if I can afford it at the time), I grab the item. If the store has rented spaces or showcases, I'll inquire about rental fees and commissions. Many have a waiting list of dealers wanting showcase space.

Remember to ask about discounts. Some dealers keep on file a list of the discounts given by type of product sold. This lets the store owner do a little bit of negotiating for bargain hunters.

ESTATE SALES AND SUCCESS STORIES

If you are fortunate, you can get on want lists or preferred customer lists with estate sales companies. Some on the preferred customer lists get good treatment, having a preview sale invitation. This means you arrive the day before the public does, therefore getting a better chance to get premium items. Having a preview means that when you go to the sale as the general public, you might be too late for the real good stuff. You need to buy stuff at these sales to get on and keep on the invite list. They do this for buying and spending customers.

Here are some stories that contain good information that you might find helpful when dealing with estate sales. These examples show what can happen before you get to a sale, which is why pre-estate sale opportunities can be so good.

A fellow I used to work with related this story to me before I got real interested in picking. He told me of how they cleaned out his folks' home in order to get ready for an estate sale. They actually had a large commercial dumpster hauled in and tossed out enough stuff to completely fill it. As he described what he tossed, we supposed there were hundreds of collectible items, including lots of old books the family had no interest in, old toys and figurines, and glassware. He also said that the day of the sale, people were fighting each other to buy stuff "just like some of the stuff we threw away!" He had no idea.

These things must happen all the time. Another person I worked with did some cleaning up before their folks' sale. The worst of it is, she didn't bother to tell anyone about the sale at work until after it was over. She said her father had an entire workshop in the basement and they took a few of the new, usable tools. They then invited the neighbor to come over and take anything he wanted.

Her father was a tile worker for many years and had stored in his basement boxes and boxes of brand new but vintage embossed tin ceiling tiles—you know the type that has all that filigree decoration you see in old turn-of-the-century buildings. They tossed it all out thinking it was just old junk. I can't imagine what a replacement antique hardware company sells them for or how much they will pay for them.

A picker I know, who is aggressive, astute, and proudly professes twenty-five years of experience in the business, often tells a story. He had an experience at an estate sale where he noticed out in the back yard a pile of about forty black garbage bags. Surely this was the stuff they cleaned up before the sale, he thought, and politely asked if he could go through the bags if he promised to not leave a mess. They said fine and asked if he would keep an eye out for a piece off of an antique that might have been thrown away by mistake.

As he searched through all of the junk, he said he found lots of old vintage windup toys, jewelry, badges, and many other collectibles. He filled up four boxes of good stuff. He also found the missing item that the family was looking for. When it was all over, he wholesaled the entire lot for $350 to a dealer. You need to now realize that the dealer sold that "garbage" for at least twice or possibly a lot higher than he paid for it. He says he's sure this happens at most of the estate sales. In fact, he says he's had similar finds in the trash many times since. Thousands of fine collectibles are tossed out in the trash every day. Another mans' trash…

Never Leave Piles Unattended

If you go to a sale and find treasures you like, you need to protect your territory and property. More than once, I have been out foraging with my wife and then discovered with a shock that her little pile was violated by another shopper. You need to realize that unless there is a big sold sticker on items, they all look like fair game. Luckily, we have been fortunate to convince the seller these were our selections and turn the sale back in our favor. After all, we saw and grabbed the items first. Once we even paid for an item downstairs, and later found it missing, only to find someone else upstairs paying for it! This can really cause fur to fly!

If you are not careful, it can ruin your day to lose out on an item you had your heart set on. It's just as bad if you cause someone else the same frustration. Always carry the stuff around with you and take it to your car after paying for it. Never leave a pile of stuff alone or it might be grabbed. After all, you saw a bargain, and it's likely someone else will also see it as a great deal.

Conducting Your Own Estate Sale

If you ever had to dispose of an estate, you know how much work is involved. I did this for my parents' estate and after reading this, hopefully you will have a better appreciation of what goes on.

After my mother and father passed away, we needed to clean the house out and divide the estate. This was all interesting for me because I had attended many similar sales and wondered what the family was going through. Of course, the first thing is dealing with the emotions and the grief of your loss. The next stage is dealing with the matters at hand like insurance, bank accounts, and other official business. The next stage is going through and finding all the memories and treasures. Then we had to decide who got what items and the work started. We sorted and organized. We tossed out lots of absolute garbage. We displayed and arranged throughout the house all of the various items. We did a lot of cleaning.

We decided to sell it ourselves. After everything was divided between my two brothers and myself and removed, we sorted, cleaned, and priced much of the stuff. I had a good friend of mine help me price the collectibles. He

TIP: If you sell the estate yourself, keep all the items worth over a certain dollar amount in the same room as the cashier. Put all items that are tiny and can be hidden in the hand in a small glass case. Only have one entrance and exit to the house or sale.

has much more expertise in certain areas I don't collect, and just charged the estate by the hour. It was helpful and I'm sure it paid off in the value of what was sold.

We listed an ad in the local daily classifieds and put up fluorescent signs on all the busy street corners and the front lawn. The morning of the sale, we had a huge crowd. Publicity was successful—security wasn't. People were jerks. They made a mess as they rummaged through the stuff. They broke stuff, and stole items. They changed price stickers on things. Negotiating is fine and in fact I encourage it, but the demands some of these people had were absolutely ridiculous.

There was a metal scrap lady who came up to me at the sale. She had a ploy I will warn you about. She came first to me and asked how much for all the metal scrap she could find. I asked her to give me a better description. We went downstairs, and she pointed out old galvanized pipes, and rods and stuff dad had. I told her to fill up a box and I'd price it. When she returned, her box had a few little pipes and a couple of the pieces she showed me, but also old turn-of-the-century door lock mechanisms, handles, and hardware. There were also chains that were attached to antique glass bowl lamps that were downstairs. She was picking for an antiques hardware supplier. What a snake!

We made some money. I even brought in some of my own personal stuff to sell, and sold a lot of it. I guess it was a success, although I don't think I'd do it that way again. But the education was valuable to me. I suppose that what we lost in selling too low and from theft or breakage, we made up in some cash, experience, and knowledge. I made some valuable contacts, too.

In doing this myself, the main thing I learned was that the people who are buying from you are a *solution*. You have to get rid of stuff. You can't and don't want to take it all. You have already separated out the memories. Now it's just stuff that's left. I also learned better as a buyer, and hope to help you have more respect for these people. It's fine as a buyer to negotiate and it's okay to get good deals, but don't insult these people or yourself with a lack of integrity and don't be dishonest. Your experience may tell you the price is cheap for something. They might just want to get rid of it at any price and be done with it.

I think in our situation, we should have hired it out to a local estate sale liquidator; yes, it would cost more, but I think we would have made it up on the other end by the extra margin they would have made on it.

Now, for you as a picker, what does this mean? You now know better what kind of estate sale you're going to: family, professional, etc. You also could, as you gain experience, offer your services either by word of mouth or by actually starting a company and advertising, etc.

HOW IS THE BEST WAY TO DO AN ESTATE SALE?

1. **DO IT YOURSELF.** This is a lot of work, no expertise; get all profit, hard to cover all the bases, messy.
2. **HIRE IT OUT TO AN ESTATE COMPANY.** They work, they get a hefty percentage, and they take care of it all.
3. **AUCTIONEER.** They do as above, but may get a lot more, or less in some cases, best security, big percentage, they handle each item, they have the best documentation, but they won't do it if the family has picked all of the good items.
4. **SELL A PIECE AT A TIME TO DEALERS.** Good luck, it would take forever, and gas mileage, time, knowledge . . . well, it wouldn't be good except for just a few items.
5. **SELL IT ONLINE.** Maybe just the top few items with value. You are dreaming if you think you can sell your parents' estate on eBay. The real estate you need to sell is way more valuable than the doodads.

If you ever see theft or dishonesty while at these sales, stop it. Help out the heirs.

Having your own estate sale is an educational event. The family is all involved and at least curious, if not anxious, to see how and what is divided. Many times there can be struggles, but fortunately, we were all pretty good with each other.

Types of Estate Sale Businesses

HIGH-GRADERS: They high grade all of the good stuff for their own collection. This is controversial, as they may have an arrangement with the family or heirs, that they take or buy a few items as part of their compensation. I would think that it would be tempting, but wonder about the ethics once in a while. I suppose it's better than outright stealing, which needs no discussion.

A LITTLE SECRET

If an estate sale is on a Friday and Saturday, sometimes you can go by the place during the previous day and find someone working to price and prepare the sale. Once in awhile, you can talk them into letting you see the stuff and maybe even buy some items before the crowds arrive. Your friends and colleagues will think you have all the luck, and won't understand how you do it.

PREMIER DEALERS: These folks only seem to choose the finest of estates. High-end furniture, high prices, probably high commissions. Likely lower sales because of the extreme prices.

LOW BALLERS: They usually have a lot of the messy estates, lots of junk, and price it low. If buying from a low baller, you can usually put together a pile and name your own price.

FAMILY RUN SALES: You need to realize the mixed feelings here. The sale is usually the result of a death in the family, and the family is just trying to get through it all. Sometimes there are some good deals because the family cannot have the experience of a seasoned dealer to know values. On the other hand, sometimes there is way too much value, and prices, because of sentimental value. "I can't sell it for any less, it was grandpa's favorite." The worst is when you have an established estate sale dealer, with a family member owner, hovering around at the sale and discussing or arguing prices and negotiations. The dealers hate it and the customers hate it. Some weird events happen with this arrangement.

ANTIQUES DEALERS: They price everything as if they are in an actual antiques store. Sometimes they have even invited an appraiser to come in. Or they look on eBay, and even print a page of what it is selling for there. They don't have a completed eBay price, just the open price, the highest priced one they could find, taped right on the item. I usually walk away from sales like this.

"FAIR" DEALERS: They have good clean organization, they have clearly marked and fairly priced items, and they even give quantity or even resellers discounts.

A table set up at an estate sale.

Like any other business, it's always good to get to know the regular dealers and their helpers. Know and use their name. Recognize them and they will recognize you. If you keep coming, they value you as a good paying customer, and they will at some point give you a break. They will also get used to your purchases, and know what you like, and either save stuff for you, or tell you where your type products are placed in the sale as you walk through the door. It's a people business. Some even invite some of their regulars to preview sales before the public comes. If you can, establish yourself as a resource to any of your known dealers, for example, if you know books very well. They just might invite you in to see what's there for your help and guidance. You may get a chance at a few items first, like we discussed earlier, or at least you'll know what's in the sale and where they are on the shelves.

Things Are Getting Weird

I went to an estate sale in town recently, thinking I would be arriving early. HA! I was number 63 in line, and people were lining up way behind me. This was for a tiny little old house. There were so many people crowded in there it was scary. I think with all the shows on TV and blogs like this telling people about all the wonders of picking, we are creating a monster. It was February and few sales were being advertised, so maybe everyone just wanted to get out for a Saturday sale, and that was all there was. I noticed the regular pickers, the dealers, who hit all the sales. I noticed a large bunch of amateurs.

I found a set or series of books that I wanted and I believe that just "because I was interested," some other guy thought they must be good, too, so he started stripping off the same shelf, the same series. He probably did not even know what they were, but knew I was interested in them. This guy kind of ticked me off and I could tell he was an amateur, but I still did pretty well considering the crowd.

Taking Children Picking

My wife and I recently took our three grandchildren with us to an estate sale. It was interesting. There were a few times where it was like trying to herd a bunch of kittens. I'm sure it bothered many of the other pickers there. My grandson likes to do magic card tricks and found a small leather wallet with some cards and dice, etc. He saw it earlier downstairs, kept thinking about it, and decided he wanted it, so I told him to go back and get it. After we got home, I said, "Let's take a look at what you bought." I opened the package and found the cards were still sealed, with tissue, and had an Internal Revenue

Service "Playing Cards" postage like stamp sealing the package. Beneath the tissue paper, you could easily read, "Buy United States Savings Bonds." He did better that day than I did. My granddaughter found a gold Cross pen and pencil set, with gold University of Utah logos on them. The logos were manufactured by O.C. Tanner Company. They make gold jewelry and items like this. She also did better than I did.

I am either creating monsters or another generation of quality antique pickers. I am also creating my own competition!

The 'Greatest' Estate Sale in the World

I didn't even want to go inside and see what was there and I walked away mad. The ad online told of the wonderful accomplishments of this fine person and how they had scoured the country for fine antiques. It told of wonderful one-of-a-kind collectibles. They warned in the ad: no phone calls, no early birds, cash only, an 8 a.m. sharp start. I was getting kind of excited.

I got to the place, got in line, and they were passing out numbers in line. They said they would allow only 12 people at a time in the house. I was number 37, so if there were any good things, and pickers were finding them, I could be out there for an hour or two. They would let another person in when one left. Within minutes, a couple came out. "Don't waste your time. It's only two rooms and everything is priced way above retail. If you are going to anymore sales this morning, you should leave now. This is a waste of time," they said. Another minute later, one of the regular pickers I know came out and had a look of shock and disgust on his face. "Worst sale I have ever seen!" he said. About this time, six or seven people in line, including myself, left the sale. I was not even curious to see what was inside.

Some people are pretty foolish when putting on a sale like this. Some may invite "appraisers" in to price everything. Nothing sells. Some are so interested in the loved one's sentimental history of something, they price it higher. Nothing sells. Some print out pages, showing what the same item sells for on eBay, and tape it to the items. Nothing sells. If they want eBay prices, they should keep sell them on eBay. Sentimental value cannot be transferred. Fame can be transferred, but it is rare, and only if you have the proof and provenance.

A Secret Way to Find Estate Sales

Here is a major secret that can give you an edge on the competition, save you gobs of time and gas money, and get you there first. Most of the time, estate sales (and yard sales) listed in the paper will have a short description to draw interest. They usually list the date and time of the sale and the address, but seldom list a phone number. Online sales will usually show a phone number.

Study the ad, highlighting all the potential good sales you want to visit. Look online to find a reverse directory. You can look up an address and find a phone number and name, or if you have a phone number only, you can find the address and name. Now, importantly, with care and tact, call the people and ask about the estate sale. If you are looking for something in particular, just ask. Most will be overwhelmed at how you could find their phone number, but just be nice and tell them you have access to a special directory. Apologize if they get upset.

Most of the time you can get a better description of the sale and what will be there. You might even get model numbers and prices on stuff they are selling. Rarely, you might even find someone who will let you come in early, maybe the evening before the sale. If they have something I really want, I've even had them hold the item for me. This way of making an early contact can save you lots of time and energy trying to check all the stops. Plus you can prioritize your highlighted stops or remove some completely.

FLEA MARKETS AND SWAP MEETS

This can be your local, every weekend meet, or in conjunction with a show somewhere. Your local swap meet is usually an "anything goes" situation. The swap meet at a show of course has a limited scope, with specialized types of materials. There are also certain regional flea markets and meets that encompass acres of land and take days to see it all. These large meets are unbelievable and you can find most anything you want. Because of the immense volume of products brought, and the enormous competition, prices are kept low. Always remember to save some money for the last day, as the prices drop sharply for product that hasn't sold. Prices are not always rock bottom at a swap meet, though; after all, most merchandise was purchased "out picking" and brought there to sell. However, sometimes you can find amazing deals at each meet you attend, as not everyone knows all of the market values of good stuff. Some of the sellers have a specialty and a good selection, which is better than random yard sales. Some swap meets are just permanent dealers, who import cheap goods from Mexico or China and sell as flea merchants, but unless you are looking for that stuff, it's a waste of time.

There are many larger cities that have flea markets, which may have some potential to find some products to resell, and may be a good outlet to sell through. One problem is the permanent "flea merchants." One time I had an opportunity to visit San Jose, California, and while there, I went to the

A tool vendor's booth at the San Jose Flea Market.

large flea market there. As a picker, I was really disappointed. It was large and in some ways interesting, but the problem for a picker, especially because I was looking for antiques and collectibles, is that they were just not there. There were hundreds of merchants selling what seemed to be the same cheap, imported stuff. There was a large area that was the fresh produce sales area, and even there, the booths were pretty much the same, that is, selling the exact same products and for the same prices. I understand that the market does open up "tailgating" areas for people to bring their junk and swap meet stuff, but it was not the weekend I attended. Unless you just want to find a bunch of cheap Chinese or Mexican imports, you are better off looking elsewhere. This was not a "picker's" venue. There were a few dealers selling second-hand tools, but I couldn't see anything of much value.

AUCTIONS

Auctions are your friend, but there are no friends at auctions. They are an exciting experience, and I emphasize experience. There's a high level of energy and emotion that accompanies an auction. Sometimes you can get an unbelievable deal at an auction. Often you can pay extremely high prices if you are not watching or planning. Planning is important, because most people cannot make good decisions quickly enough while the auctioneer is spouting off. The fervor is what drives the selling of the goods. The same goods can sit for weeks and months in a dealer's shop or booth and never sell at a better price than at some bid prices.

People can't stand the fact that others will get a good deal and they themselves lose out. This pride is the engine that moves the auction along. Watch the auctioneer and learn how he or she does it. Sometimes he or she lets items go quite low just to get things going. The auctioneers control the bidders.

When you arrive at an auction, you will generally see items sorted into numbered lots, which are usually the same types of products. You will also see a marvelous assortment of people. I usually see dealers and pickers recognized at other places. You will see people taking lots of notes and whispering to each other. Some have cell phones and make calls and take photos, I assume to get a sale before the auction starts, but more likely to get permission from someone at home to buy.

The auction starts and there are many fast decisions made. Sometimes there are good deals, sometimes not. People are pleased or disappointed. Some have regrets that they won; some have regrets that they lost.

I remember an auction where the auctioneer kept it going with myself and another bidder in the back of the room. He got me quite high before I finally bought it. I never did turn around to see whom I was bidding against. There's always a possibility there really was not a bidder behind me. Nah, that doesn't really happen, does it?

I know that regular attending bidders or the old pros at certain government auctions are said to bid newcomers way up, and then let them buy it way too high in order to discourage them from encroaching onto their territory. Often the novice sees their error, and leaves without paying for the stuff, and the old pro has a chance to pick it up on a later bid time or date.

It's loads of fun to win a bid for a whole section of product or a "lot" that you did not have a chance to completely inspect. You then get to search through it, finding fun treasures and surprises. You should always look over the merchandise carefully while the pressure is off. This is usually at a preview time the day before. Take good notes and read them over in a quiet time before the auctioning starts. Decide beforehand what you really wish to buy, and how much is the price you would like along with the highest price you would pay. Be sure you have the money! Realize if you bid and win, it's yours. They usually always require cash.

Try to ignore the excitement. You're simply there for a good deal. If someone else wants to pay a high price, they deserve what they get. What I want is a good deal. The item you might lose may be a "one of a kind," but there is always countless "one of a kinds" out there. Yes, there are good opportunities, but you have to plan and think quickly. If you want it, get it. No one is nice to the other guy. This business is not for the timid. Remember: You have a 50/50 chance at the auction—you either get the item or you don't.

Storage Unit Auctions

First of all, don't believe what you see on television. These shows are entertainment only. The actors seem so surprised at what they find, which is amazing, since items are placed by the reality TV production company. Real storage unit auctions can be a lot of fun. There are online sources that do list upcoming storage auctions by state and city, but it's too bad this "fun" is at someone else's expense—when you rent a storage unit, you sign an agreement that says you will let the landlord sell your property if you don't pay your bill. They advertise and sell the items at whatever someone is willing to bid. Usually a small crowd gathers around and the unit is opened; you look at it from the outside, not able to pick through or inspect it. You just look in and make your bid. The winner gets it all and removes it that day or the next. You get the treasure and the junk. The sale is usually fairly informal, with minimal competition, and the items are varied and interesting. You will need to bring cash; if you don't, the next highest bidder will get it immediately. You must also bring a powerful flashlight, since sometimes you can hardly see into the back of the unit, and your flashlight may save you.

'Salted' Auctions

I was excited to see in the newspaper a major auction in our local area. The large ad told of an amazing assemblage of collections from millions of dollars in oriental rugs to glassware and antique furniture, to gold, silver, and countless priceless items. It was to be held in an exclusive home that was also to be auctioned off.

My wife and I went to the auction and after a quick search, found that this was nothing more than a sales organization with a fantastic, but deceiving, way to confuse the public into paying too much for worthless junk. They had large mahogany antiqued furniture, vases, glassware, rugs, and quilts, but it was all decorator items. It was stuff they imported from India and China, and they removed the country of origin labels from the items and auctioned them off. There were large bronzes after Remington, which tells me they were counterfeits. What a scam. This was what is called a "salted" auction. Any coins, silver, and antiques that were there were nothing more than a few goodies they bought at a coin shop or an antique store to make the place look good.

They did the whole thing in cahoots with a local realtor, who found a way to get hundreds of people through the house she had listed. They had employee "plants," who looked like they were there as buyers, making fake "shill" bids to increase the selling price. I'm sure the unlucky bidders got their treasures home and found out much too late that they had bought cheaply made, but expensive, decorations. By then, the auction company would be long gone, doing it to someone else in another city.

OTHER GOOD PLACES TO PICK

CLUBS AND SPECIALTY SHOWS. A show can be an enjoyable, educational, and profitable experience. This is where everybody comes out. The biggest dealers have booths selling the best products, and you also see the best-of-the-best items. You can gain much knowledge and association in these events. People are enthusiastic and ready to buy, sell, and trade. The fun and excitement are all part of the experience. Sometimes a club breathes interest in your topic, which helps the economy grow for your items. (Hype+Fervor=Value!) You not only make good deals, but you can make valuable friends and contacts. If you don't have a local club or show for your special products, you could start one yourself. I know of an aggressive picker who formed a club so he can move the stuff he picks over the months. Wise move.

GARAGE SALES. Also called yard sales, tag sales, or even moving and divorce sales. This is about individuals selling unwanted stuff in hopes of getting a little cash. Most of the time, this is not your best place to spend a lot of effort. Lots of clothing and junk is usually put out. There are exceptions, though, and some wonderful surprises. If they advertise something in your specialty or if you are on your way somewhere, it might surprise you what you might find. I usually like to go "yard sailing" on my way home from estate sales.

SURPLUS STORES. These can be various types of stores, surplus, army/navy, electronics, or otherwise. You might find some good bargains at these stores. They are great places to "poke around" because stuff is usually piled randomly and obscured by other junk and packaging. Also many universities have some surplus stores that sell to the public. You can find anything from file cabinets to scientific equipment. You might even have a local state, federal, or military surplus agency nearby that you should check out. Often they hold large auctions where you can find interesting and valuable merchandise.

FREIGHT-DAMAGED OUTLETS. These usually handle newer products, such as items that may have been bought in "lot" quantities by brokers. They are good to check out occasionally and be familiar with. You may be able to sell some of these items to people you see advertising what they want in certain classified ads.

SALVAGE YARDS. Some cities have salvage operations that harvest windows, doors, and all sorts of architectural treasures from home and building demolition. You never know what you might find here. They may also be a good customer for any antique building hardware you come across. Ask what types of things they look for and how much they pay.

FACTORIES AND LOCAL MANUFACTURERS. Some manufacturers have surplus items for sale, which could be parts, finished units, demo units, defects, or testing and inspection equipment. An example could be a semiconductor manufacturer that occasionally disposes of a group of inspection microscopes. I've been involved in similar deals, which have been profitable. They also occasionally have office furnishings and supplies. Many times the employees get first dibs, but call and ask.

COLLECTORS. Always try and make contact with as many collectors as you can. These are good sources for product as well as great customers. As you get familiar with their specialties, interests, and wants and they with yours, you can make some good deals and trades.

BOOK FAIRS, LIBRARY SALES, BOOK STORES. Find out when and where all of the good used book sales are. If you pick for anything in particular, there are usually books written on your subject. Some libraries have "friends" sales to dispose of excess and duplicate books. You need to always ask if they have a preview sale for members, and find out how to become a member if they do. The preview sale is where all of the good stuff is. **Note:** volunteers and employees probably have a preview before anyone. Many used bookstores are also places to find a treasure or two. They can't possibly know the value of every book, especially in obscure markets that you may have.

OTHER SOURCES AND PLACES TO SELL. There are many places and people to sell to including museums, other pickers, dealers, friends, relatives, fellow employees, neighbors, etc. Ask around and tell people what you do. Get the word out and do some good networking. Some of the best once-in-a-lifetime deals come from friends. Word of mouth is how you find those pre-estate sales and private collections. These are all without competition and with better prices and often friends and relatives give you stuff.

NATIONAL SOURCES. Get familiar with dealers who advertise nationally. Send for catalogs; in fact, get on all kinds of mailing lists. Look forward to certain types of junk mail. Peruse and study different types of information sent to be familiar with all sorts of products. Start collecting catalogs, especially vintage ones, as you come across them. Be aware of parts and service sources. This is great training material for prices, too.

MAGAZINES AND CLASSIFIEDS. Magazines, especially those that cover your particular specialty, can be valuable sources of information. You can gain a great education and working knowledge of your topic by reading every month. You can also harvest countless great contacts from these. Remember to circle those little bingo cards to get lots of information sent to you.

THE INTERNET. This subject is way too big to discuss, but by all means, get on the Internet. You can bid on anything you wish to buy, or you can sell almost anything you can get on the auction and store services such as eBay, Etsy, Amazon, etc. You can search and advertise on Google groups. Be involved in forums that discuss your specialty. You can get on certain email mailing lists for just about any topic. You should bookmark as many applicable web pages and find as many links as you can to pages relating to your specialty. Learn how to use the search engines. You can also design and post your own web page to market your products and to find stuff. WordPress is a great way to get started. If you don't have a clue of what I describe here, go find out. Get a good book or go to a class, and then try it.

PAWN SHOPS. You might just be able to find a few prizes here, although I personally haven't found much at these stores. It seems that the prices are quite high on many items—even higher than at antiques stores and malls.

Besides, you have to make your way through all of the guns, guitars, jackhammers, socket wrenches, and big-carpeted speakers to find anything. But, there are things to be found if you look far enough. Some people who get in good with the shop owners get great bargains. I know someone who has a relative working at a pawnshop. The owner will call him first when any of the items my friend is looking for are brought in. This might be why I don't see any items that interest me because there are people buying the good stuff— "up stream feeding" I like to call it.

SECOND-HAND/THRIFT STORES. These can range from the tiny converted house or small strip mall shop to the large almost department store variety. They usually exist from donations of used, no longer wanted items. Some have a relationship with certain worthy causes, such as church welfare or veterans or handicapped organizations. The profits can be used to provide relief, to help train and motivate, to feed, cure, etc. The stores are usually non-profit in nature. There are some smaller thrift stores that exist as profitable ventures to their owners, and the crazy thing is, that they still receive donations.

THE IMPORTANCE OF SIGNS

Whether it's for an estate sale, yard sale, garage sale, or tag sale, signs are really important. Addresses are pretty hard to find sometimes, but GPS systems really help. The big problem is the "regular" yard sale signs. If you are planning a yard sale, you may place an ad in the paper, or on Craigslist or some other favorite local online site. Always double-check it, and realize that a large percentage of people will attend the sale by only seeing the sign at the last minute.

The best possible sign is placed strategically on nearby main roads, and the markings must be large and bold to be seen from a moving vehicle. I have seen signs with one-inch sharpie letters that you need to get out of your car to read. The ideal lettering should be with the widest most ridiculous-sized black permanent marker you can find. If you only have a thin one, thicken the letters. I would hope the letters to be three to four inches high, and the line width to be at least 1/4 inch to 3/8 inch thick. Don't put too much information on the sign. Many look like kids wrote them, and they are going to make lots of money that day, so they list all the items mom told them they need to sell. I also like when the seller puts small arrows made from the same color poster board, showing the various turns, and helps you find your way there. I saw a great sign recently that just said, "In the yellow house on the corner." We found it and my wife bought something from the sale.

There were great signs leading all the way to one particular sale I once attended, but unfortunately, it wasn't the best sale.

Sellers, you need to realize there are usually some pretty important sales that same day. The diehard pickers, scouts, and dealers head there first. They may stop on the way to the big sale, if it's clear to them where you are. A good picker will hit all the major estate sales, and then might go "yard sailing" on the way back, that is, finding yours and other sales along the way. Make it easy for everybody.

It's also important to remember that when the sale is finished to take down your signs. It is so wasteful in time and gas, and frustration, to go the next week and find that you are a week late. Never advertise a yard sale as an estate sale. I have followed signs to some of the lamest garbage garage sales that claimed they were estate sales. I have been led to "estate sales" that are just junk stores posing as a sale, but hold this same estate sale every week or so.

GOLD!

Ever since I have been picking for antiques and collectibles, I have found gold teeth four times. On a recent day, it was in a prescription bottle that contained nine grams of dental gold. I had gathered together a couple of books on geology, two old slide rules, a pocket knife, and some hardware, and this old prescription bottle. I laid it on the cashier table at the estate sale. The man said, "Hmmm, how about five dollars?" When I weighed it out and figured that gold today is over $1,600 per troy oz., and nine grams is about .28 troy oz., and the gold value estimate of dental gold could be 75 percent, it came out to $344.

I let the seller set the price. I did not hide the items. They were all there to be seen. But, I ask you, was this dishonest or unethical?

Years ago, I bought a large and important collection of minerals and crystals from someone that included some wonderful and rare pieces, including a pretty valuable "Thatcher's Rule," which is like a big cylindrical slide rule. I bought it for $100. I sold it for $600. I went back and gave the person I got it from another $200 after I received my payment. The guy I sold it to then sold it for $1,500. Was anyone in the wrong here? Does ethics have any business at all in the picking business? Even the famous *American Pickers* on TV have some controversy online about their escapades.

Does it have to be gold? Is that too blatant of a find? What if you find cash in an old book? What if you find any kind of item that you know is impossibly rare, but it is so obscure and esoteric, and the chances are you are the only one in a hundred square miles knows anything about it? If you buy it cheap, are you taking advantage or just a smart businessperson? After all, you "paid" for your knowledge. Is that any different than a doctor knowing more about how to cut into you? He is adding value to the situation because of his education.

CRAIGSLIST: THE ONLINE PICKER'S MONEY MAKER

As an antiques picker, I used to live by what was in the newspaper yard sale, garage sale, estate sale, and other sale ads. Everything has changed. The local paper is old news when it comes to estate sales. Most of my information is found online. Craigslist and other sites have all the ads. Even if there happens to be a dealer or a family who place an ad in the paper, you'll find it online first. It's too bad. Actually, it's too bad the paper does not list these sales for free. The only reason they are online, and not in the paper, is people are cheap, and so they seek "free." Free Internet ads have replaced the printed classifieds. If they had free classifieds for these categories, I'd subscribe. I'm sure many others would, too. While they are at it, come up with some better categories instead of mixing all the estate sales with the yard sales.

We have a local radio and TV station that has had free ads for as long as the Internet has been around. People here really use the service. It's almost like a local eBay for free. Check in your area and see if something similar is happening.

Recently I bought a $750 Glass Fusing Kiln from a Craigslist ad. He was in Montana and I was in Utah. We both drove halfway and met in Idaho Falls, Idaho. I had already talked him down from $1,000, so I figured I paid for my gas. He hadn't sold it as soon as he hoped, and was willing to pay his own gas to get my cash.

Craigslist sells millions of product constantly. If you are a Power Seller on eBay, like I am, you will still do well to sell on Craigslist. You save commissions and listing fees. You can ask for and receive cash, and save PayPal fees. You can sell large items that are difficult to package and ship.

Technical antiques such as these especially appeal to male buyers.

Chapter 5

....

Falling into Good Deals Takes Planning

My father declared once, "I don't see how you 'fall into' so many good deals."

I guess it's like falling into a mineshaft. In order to fall into it, you have to be near the mine. In order to be near the mine, you have to have a map showing you where it is. You might need to have someone take you there. You need the right vehicle to get you to the mine and have all the right equipment to collect. In other words, you have to plan to "fall into" the good deals. You have to do lots of prospecting. You need to talk to people. You need to pass out cards and get exposure. You have to follow up on leads and hunches. If you have more irons in the fire, you have more hot deals!

ANTIQUES CLASSIFIEDS

There are many antiques and collectibles magazines, newsletters, and periodicals available, which can be of general interest, as well as special interest publications and sites. Some of the magazines you get you will wish to keep and collect all copies for reference. Some have timely and perishable information; others have good material to refer to over the years. You can find dozens of good contacts as you read through the publications. You should organize these contacts in a special written file or computer file by topics, wants, or interest, so it's convenient to refer to when you find something you need to sell or talk to an expert about, etc.

There are also countless specialized forums online to bookmark when you come across them. For online forums listing "buy and sell" ads, you will want to frequent often, and make comments and posts, so people get to know you.

This all helps you when you have an opportunity to buy something but want to pre-sell it—that is, find a customer before you purchase it or even bid on it. More often than not, these contacts will give you wonderful information on what to look for, watch out for, and even give you ball-park appraisals. Your phone call just might result in a good profit, save you from a disaster, or help you avoid bad deals.

When you contact someone, you could approach it this way: "I saw your ad in an edition of X. I recently came across in a thrift store a X, model ABC. I know you deal in this stuff and I need your help. I'll probably keep it for myself, but I don't know. They want $X for it; is that too much to pay?"

You might get responses this:

- "I'm sorry. I do not give appraisals over the phone." (This is probably a poor contact).
- "If you can get it for $100, I'll double your money." (This could be good for you, but make sure you work out arrangements like freight, payment, etc. up front).
- "No. If you buy it for $100, they're ripping you off. Hey, I'll sell them to you for that." (Good helpful contact, thanks for the help!)
- "Well, you have to be careful. Some models have a broken X you can tell right off if it's the good one everybody wants, because it has an X or, only the red ones have any collectible value ..." (This is a great contact and valuable information you are receiving, and it makes you an expert. You should work with this contact in the future and develop a good dealer/picker relationship. Buy stuff from and sell to this person.)
- "No, you should call such and such company—they are the experts." (Thank them for their honest help and find out what they specialize in while you're on the phone; you never know where it will lead.)

If they know they're probably not going to have a chance at buying what you have or if they're not interested right then, they will probably be pretty honest with the valuation they give. You might hear an answer like, "You paid $5? Yeah, it's a good deal. We sell them all day long for at least $30 each in any condition."

Here's how you might begin the picker/dealer relationship: Tell them you see this sort of stuff often and ask what prices they pay pickers for it. Some might only offer paying you double what you pay, but guarantee to buy all you find. Others will gladly pay you "keystone" or one half, or the going retail price. Search for good dealers who always seem to have the money and are willing to buy what you find.

Keystone—is that fair? One half of the retail price? If an item is "worth" a hundred bucks, why don't you hold out for the full bore price? First of all, can you afford to wait for the money? Remember the law of turnover. You make more money on turning your dollars over and keeping cash as a fluid, working power, than by holding on trying to make a bit more profit. This dealer you work with does the same thing. He or she has to turn over the entire inventory a certain amount of times to realize any profit. This extra the dealer makes by selling retail is worth it, too, because of the overhead they have that you don't. The dealer might have rent and advertising and utilities and store fixtures that he pays for that you don't have to worry about.

If you buy something for a dollar and sell it for ten times that amount, and then see that the dealer doubles that price, is it fair? You bet it is. As long as he can keep selling these things at this high price, he'll keep buying stuff from you. (Your increase was pretty good, too, remember?) As you get closer to the dealer, you also get more information because they will tell you more about what they want and tips, etc. This is free training. Make sure you write it down and review it.

Make sure of how much material they can use. You might just buy too much and be stuck with inventory. Realize that styles, fads, and tastes all change. Have them tell you what is needed to protect the products for shipping, storage, etc. Care and cleaning tips are also invaluable.

Within your card index, you should have a specific "want list" that goes a bit beyond the list of contacts by topic or experts. This comes from the various dealers, collectors, and others you find advertised or even spoken wants you hear. You can start with the specialties you are particularly interested in and later add all different types of subjects. You might be interested in furniture. You could list others who buy furniture and sort it by series or period. As mentioned, you could then add those looking for furniture, hardware, or books, etc. As you go along, add art, toys, or other book topics. After all, you will be out and about, and find all kinds of things while you are looking for your items. This way you will have a resources list and a potential customer file. You can then "pick" for these other folks and make extra funds to pursue your own specialty.

This can be an interesting and powerful tool. You can be as elaborate as you wish, entering all the contacts into a computer database, or you could be as simple as having a card or computer file.

TICKLER FILE

This is a separate file you keep for all of those leads you find or people give you to "check out one of these days." You should follow up on some as soon as you can, where others could possibly wait. Every time you have a good idea, inspiration, or overhear some great tip, put it here. You may find lots of excellent leads as you get into this business, but unless you keep track of them, they are lost, so you need to develop a "tickler file." Do you want to be the one to close the big deals? If you want to be successful buying and selling estates and collections, or even just pick and sell, you need to check back regularly and have lots of deals cooking. Literally, some deals can take years to complete. Estates may lay dormant, people stay undecided, change their minds, or may not be ready to sell various properties.

You might be fortunate and have a friend who is watching out for you and gives you a good lead. Or you might just be lucky and fall into information of some items you like for sale. Better yet, you may be advertising for these items and someone answers the ad. Sometimes it's a garage, a basement, a storage unit, or an entire house of stuff you are anxiously looking for. It might be just one item that is valuable and unique.

You contact the owner or the heir and it might just come together. Because it sounds so positive and hopeful, you still need to check back; someone else could easily "scoop" you—even if it looks as if there is no competition.

Often people forget, lose your name and number, or can't recall the details of the deal (money, list of items you want, etc.). What's really discouraging is to find out someone else firmed up the deal while you put off calling.

If you can, leave a printed business card with your interests and date written on it. This will be a reminder to your "client." Next write it in your tickler file. The tickler file you use could be a list or cards or even a calendar or day planner.

You'll be absolutely amazed how many deals you'll get before the competition even knows there was one, and your colleagues and buddies will be dumbfounded about how you seem to be the best picker in your field.

RESTORATION ADDS VALUE

You can learn how to fix and clean stuff, but if you really want to gain a skill, don't just repair, but actually restore if possible. Collectors and dealers never like to see any kind of obvious modifications, but a true restoration adds so much more value to an item. If it is a valuable piece, make sure you know what you are doing or leave it to a qualified person to do. Most serious collectors want to do their own restorations, so be careful.

SPILLING SECRETS

People like to boast and brag. It's interesting what pride does to people. You might want to try a little research like I did to write this book and see what I mean. Pretend that you are a reporter gathering information for a research project. Talk to people and ask them questions. You will be flabbergasted to see how much they will tell. They may be keeping back secrets consciously in a way, but be telling you exactly what you want in a different way. For example, they may keep secret the location they found an important item, but then tell you of how they negotiated for the item. Or they will tell you flat out how they went about finding the source for something good, a way you never considered before, giving you what should have been the most protected information and secrets. They often will give you valuable pricing tips. They may tell you what styles are most popular, etc. They will tell you of items that are now collectible that you were not aware of, and their value. Now you have another item to look for when you are searching.

If you are specializing in one area and they know it, but you ask about one of their other interests, they really open up. After all, they don't feel you're a competitor as much. But you are learning. Ask questions like, "So who buys all that glassware you find?" They will probably tell you right off, so write it in your card file. Another question might be, "So, who is the best person to talk to about this style of furniture?" Pickers all know each other. Break into the business by asking questions. You'll find it's a small world.

Many pickers, understanding the importance of quality restorations, won't do much more than light cleaning or gluing of broken pieces, but then sell it to waiting dealers who specialize in restoring. It is good to know what kind of cleaners will work on various products you handle; for example, those items made of plastic or items painted long ago. Decals and intricate paint should not be touched if at all possible. One absolutely horrible thing that even some experienced antiques dealers do is to brush rusted metal with a wire wheel—that leaves a distinctive texture on the metal. Then they simply paint it black.

'COLLEGE OF PICKING KNOWLEDGE'

When you are out picking, you are constantly learning. Every day is different. I suppose that's why people stick with this. There are so many different and interesting things. When you're looking for stuff, you may find items you have seen before or something completely new to you. This new item may show you evidence to believe it is old, rare, or expensive. So what do you do?

1. You might plunk down the cash and take it.
2. If you can, get the seller to hold it for 24 hours—but they have to keep it out of sight from other potential buyers.
3. If you really like it, want it, have the room for it, and can afford it, then purchase it.
4. If you can make a phone call to an expert or especially a potential buyer, do so, but please remember caller ID. I once made the mistake of calling a collector from another collector's house about an item. They were not aware of each other before that time.
5. If it is cheap and you can afford to lose the investment, just buy the thing.
6. If you do walk away from it, at the very least, try and find out about the thing later now that you have had the experience. Go look it up online or in a price guide, talk to an expert, or check out a dealer who may have some. You will then know more for next time. Who knows, if it is a good piece, you may discover later on that it could very well still be there. It's happened.

This is all part of the learning. This is your "college of picking knowledge." You buy books, read, and study. You pay tuition by buying and investing, and you have tests by winning some and losing some.

It ruins the piece. Some wonderful books on refinishing are available if you really want to study the correct way. Have a real good talk with each of your dealer friends and possible customers, asking what you should or shouldn't do. Find out in what kind of condition they prefer you to bring it to them.

POLISH YOUR PICKING PROFESSIONALISM

To be a professional when it comes to picking, you have to be an expert in one or more of the fields on the items you pursue. You might already be an expert in various subjects because of a job or training. You may have a strong interest in something you've casually read or just thought about, that now you really want to study. You might have a talent in an area that has a valuable history, and has items related that you want to find. You also may have collected some things as a child that you are ready to brush the dust off of in the attic. Some people may have a geographical advantage, living in an area that has a lot of interesting and important memorabilia or artifacts that can still be found, or have historical industry products that were produced locally in the past.

Become an expert! Find out what your hot button is and then find out everything you possibly can about it. Go to the library, visit museums, manufacturers, distributors, and local or nearby shows, and special meets. Frequent dealers and stores dealing in the items. See if there is a club or association in your area and get involved. Talk to old timers in the field—they have wonderful knowledge. Subscribe to newsletters and magazines and buy collector's guides to your products. Search the Internet; you'll get unbelievable amounts of information, ideas, and leads.

START READING AND RESEARCHING

Jack of all trades, but expert of none? Start a library and read. Picking is not just for antiques and knickknacks. It can be for industrial equipment and other valuable items, too. Find out about all sorts of stuff. I send for catalogs from both home and work and thumb through as many as I can. I look at machinery, hardware, tools, and what-cha-ma-call-its. I see how they are shaped and built and try to figure out what they do. I've always been interested in equipment, tools, and industries. I've always liked to either take apart stuff or fix broken things.

I scan the books and catalogs so I can learn how and with what things are done. As a result, I have profited well when out picking. I also find I am more of an expert in my work and to others because of my knowledge of things. So now when I'm at a swap meet or other likely spot and find a gadget or thing-amajig and it's a dollar or two, I pick it up. I know who uses them and I bet I can sell it. I've bought an expensive piece of test equipment for just $25 and sold it a week later for $1,200.

Get familiar with brand names. Find out which are the most expensive and why. Ask around. "I see some of the same names show up all the time when

I'm out picking, what should I be watching for?" People will ask. They want you to know because there is a better possibility to buy something you find for a good deal.

All of this works for antiques, collectibles, industrial equipment, and just about anything.

You might even get a file cabinet (when you're out picking, of course) and start a literature file of catalogs that interest you for reference. This is good to have for pricing guides, too.

As you study and immerse yourself in the subject, you'll add knowledge, gain appreciation, and become an expert quickly. You will also see how various industries and products are connected. This helps you identify items you come across. Even just looking at pictures will help you.

Try and visit various libraries in your area; university and other major libraries are especially helpful. These institutions carry many rare and out-of-print books and publications you'll never see otherwise. Some even sell or trade their old and duplicate books. Research at the library should include magazines and industrial publications, too. You'll find contacts for suppliers, dealers, and distributors in your field. See what your local library has in antiques and collectibles resource guides. Usually you will find shelves full of current books. You will also be fortunate if you find older out-of-print guides and information, which is valuable when researching certain finds.

As you also study, find the *Thomas Register* (a thirty-volume catalog approximately 8-10 feet long of just about everything) at the library. They also have a searchable database online. You will see the value of this and other references when pricing, buying, or selling stuff you're finding. You can then find many contacts, especially with toll-free numbers, to use when reference is needed. Put these names in your contact directory. You can call companies listed in the *Thomas Register* and ask who are dealers and distributors for stuff you find locally. You can also ask for current prices on items still made. Some of these listed companies buy back products, refurbish, and re-market them. They could refer you to the local distributor or dealer to buy your items.

If you find a box of widgets, call around to find the regular selling price and then offer them for one half or one-third to the dealer. They may buy them all, giving you a healthy profit. I have been involved in these types of deals often. Many folks do this and make a good living.

You can also find sources for parts, manuals, literature, etc. As you are out and come across items, you will find you have more contacts to help you sell to or just get pricing information so you can sell locally.

The more you read, the more reference material you have, and the more you study, the more success you'll have. You'll be further ahead of your competi-

A grouping of early radio items on display at an antiques show. After I became interested in vintage radios, I learned everything I could about them.

tion, enjoy it more, and find much better products. There is probably a correlation between the dollars you make and the time you study. I wish I could tell you how many dollars an hour you increase for every hour you read.

Realize, though, that books, magazines, ads, manuals, and paper on collectibles are also collectible, so find out more before you cut up old outdated information. I sell lots of new and old books on Amazon and other online book venues, as well as on eBay. New collectors coming into the field love to get out-of-print magazines and journals on the items they collect. Some even place ads for old issues wanted in order to put together a set, etc.

You should begin buying and picking for books in your specialty or various specialties. Never pass up any books on various antiques or collectibles. These will be a valuable reference. Besides, picking for books is lucrative. You'll always be able to sell them if you find they are of no use to you. Other valuable references are the historical catalogs and books on the history of your field. Vintage catalogs from manufacturers and distributors have loads of wonderful information. You can find model numbers, photos, original prices, parts and accessories, etc. These old catalogs are valuable and sought by collectors. You can sell them easily. Also look for the histories of industries, companies, and biographies of those individuals important to your particular specialty.

BECOMING AN EXPERT CAN BE EASIER THAN IT SOUNDS:

1. Be interested in something. Have a thirst for more knowledge on the topic.
2. Know its "application." This could be need or resource motivated.
   NEED: My son wants to play guitar... Learn about brands, amps, tube amps, reverbs, etc. You will become an expert.
   RESOURCE: The area you live in could have been the original manufacturing site for marbles, radios, etc., which would be a prime resource for collecting items in this special field. You will become an expert.
3. When you find something good, you research it and find out more about the topic. You will see more again later and now know more about it. You will become an expert.
4. Instant "expert." Sometimes just listening to other pickers waiting in line to go into a sale or when they are bragging outside about what they found makes you start being an expert. Your natural curiosity will take over. You will become an expert.

These things will open more doors for you.

ANTIQUES AND COLLECTIBLES PRICE GUIDES

When I started this business, I really got excited about price guides and thought that they were like manufacturers' cost books. Not hardly. The first reason a price guide is written is for the author to establish they are some sort of expert. The prices for the most part are only a guess. The real value of an item is what you can sell it for. Price guides can be useful for learning about various topics of collectibles, and the photos are important. If the author has described the items, and listed correct model numbers or names of items it is invaluable. If the writer goes further and lists the variations, tips, and warnings, then they are in fact experts, and the reference is important. Pricing changes and fluctuates often. eBay and other online venues has been a major engine of change for all antiques and collectibles. Amazon and other bookselling sites have rocked the bookstore business irreversibly. Even if you look at past auctions on eBay, you only get a recent window of pricing history.

There are tools such as Terapeak and others that can give you longer history information, but there is a price for this information.

What I like to do is keep a collectibles journal. It's nothing more than a small address booklet with letter tabs. I save a favorite search on many of the items I either wish to buy or want history on. As an item comes up on auction and I am notified, I "watch" the item. The closing bid amount is in my "watched items" list in My eBay and is kept there for as long as I wish. Once in a while, I will transfer the closing bid prices on these favorite searches into my index, by brand and part number, etc. As more items come up for bid, I keep the journal going, until I have a *real price guide*. This is now a pocket-sized spotter's list for when I go picking for things. I am now the expert. I talk more about price guides in Chapter 8.

ONE OF MY READERS SAID: *Great idea with the journal. I regularly watch eBay auctions, either with intent to buy/bid or out of curiosity. I don't know why it never occurred to me to keep a notebook. Will come in handy at estate sales/auctions, when you don't want/have time to pull out your phone and do a small research project. I'm going to include things I see quite often at estate sales, things that I know are popular collectibles, but I don't know much about. At a recent sale, there were a couple of boxes full of '40s-'50s head vases. I don't collect them, but knew that plenty of others do, and that I could probably sell them at a decent price. Well, didn't know enough about cost to buy any, so had to pass, and came home to research, I missed out. Not again!*

BE SELECTIVE

When I first started in the collecting hobby, I felt I was way too late. I saw or read about huge collections. I would study magazines and catalogs from dealers who had unbelievable stuff and lots of items. I even remember having a conversation with a nationally known dealer of certain antiques and telling him I felt like a latecomer. I said it looks like all the good stuff is gone. He was surprised at my statement. I was surprised that he was surprised. He assured me that it was just starting. He said more and more good stuff is coming out now more than ever and that he was thrilled and excited about what has been coming available on the market lately.

Be careful. There is a big temptation, especially when you are new, to buy everything in sight related to your newfound field of interest. If you don't specialize, you'll end up with lots of junk, less room, less cash, and bewilderment. Remember, there are many good deals out there, more than you can imagine. You need to continually upgrade and trade off. Turn your treasures over. I say treasures because there is the tendency to consider many old items as irreplaceable.

The tendency is to hoard everything. Some gather the good, complete, valuable products, as well as the broken down, damaged junkers.

You might need a few replacement parts and so it may be wise to hang onto certain sets to cannibalize and repair the better one that comes along.

When you get larger amounts and wonder what to do, you will want to specialize. You'll want only a certain brand, style, or date. Another great idea is to set certain value limits; for example, not collecting or dealing in anything less than $100 in book value. You then sell off, trade off, or dump the lesser stuff as you can. You'll be surprised at what your collection or inventory will look like.

AESTHETICS

Besides rarity and quality, aesthetics is the highest reason for increased value in a collectible. Understanding aesthetics is both innate and learned. You have in you a certain like and dislike for the looks of things. Those who have a real gift also do well in home decoration and display. You either have an eye for it or you don't. Now don't despair if you don't, as some of it can be learned. If you are picking for certain items, you can always memorize all the types of the hot pieces that are popular. A bit of caution: You may have the eye for it, but really want the thing—then it's going to be difficult to sell it. Or you don't have the eye for it and sell important and valuable items much too easily. Find out what stuff sells for and who wants it. Especially go for the things you want and find out why everybody wants it.

If you have ever seen a Christie's auction catalog, it's interesting how value is added to the products that will be auctioned by listing "important" in the title. For example, Christie's could just say "antique toys" and you think one thing, but when they say "important antique toys," it seems to infer lots of other possibilities, such as if it is the first ones like it ever made or maybe they were owned by famous children and they have the documents to prove it. They might have been used in a movie as props. Whatever the case, important they are, and they will sell for a bundle.

Things you look for to judge its condition: Is the case cracked? Is it in the original package? Are all of the original papers with it? Do you have any letters to and from the factory proving ownership and history? (Provenance) Is the finish original or repainted? We've all heard the stories, like the extremely valuable furniture piece that lost most of its value because the owner didn't like the original finish and so stripped and re-finished the entire piece. I have heard of items worth an original $100,000 being worth only $10,000 because of a botch job like this.

Marbles are an interesting collectible, but you need guidance from books and other collectors about what to look for, as some new marbles look old and old marbles look new. You also need to know the difference between handmade and machine-made marbles.

You have to know if it is ethical or moral to restore the item, or whether to leave it alone. When in doubt, by all means leave it alone. Are replacement or reproduction parts available for the unit? Could they have been used on this one? Is the serial number significant?

SNAP SHOTS

I call it taking snap shots. It's when you go out picking and take your chances according to your timing. Most pickers move around. You try lots of different places—ones you either just want to check out or places where you've had success in the past. You never know what is going to be put out for sale. You never know where your competition is, and remember that your competition doesn't necessarily have to be another picker or dealer that is after the stuff you want; it might just be lots of regular people that take a fancy to something you're searching for and buy it on an impulse.

This business is cyclical. It's wonderful one day or one place, and will change to nothing somewhere else or at a different time. People dispose of items randomly. Don't get discouraged if you don't find anything one day. Just by checking, you'll be that much closer to the next find. Besides, if you don't find anything, this means you still have your money. I've found myself several times buying an item at a thrift shop that I know just came out of the back room. I picked it up, paid for it, carried it out to the car, and most of the people that ever came into the store that day never saw the item. This happens many times a day. You'll look around and see a bunch of the same old stuff but realize you didn't see the best of it—it's gone. But then on your next trip, you will find the prize and they will never see it. That is why I call it a snap shot.

WHAT TO LOOK FOR BESIDES AESTHETICS

- Historical importance
- Rarity or limited production
- Beauty and finest quality (heft, and detail, and workmanship)
- Resale value
- Certain color or certain series
- Fads and trends fame (for example, it may be hot now because it was just featured in a magazine)

An actual photographic snap shot is a brief period of time that is recorded. Just like in a real photograph, you don't get the whole story. As you pick, you don't know what you'll miss.

PARLAYING

Parlaying basically means to take something and make it worth more. Say I take a dollar out of my pocket, buy something, and sell it for $5. I then take the $5 and buy an item with it, which I in turn sell for twenty dollars. I am parlaying, or building upon my original investment of one dollar. I keep adding my original and subsequent profits—in effect betting the winnings.

There is high risk in doing this, but there are also large rewards. You might discover that the sell time increases with the higher-valued items. You will also learn quickly how quality fits into the equation.

I have heard of similar stories, but instead of parlaying to different items, you track the same item through different dealers. I heard a lady at an antiques show say some dealers were selling some highly valued collectible from collector and dealer to collector, etc. for the entire week. It ended up selling in the end for a hundred dollars less than it started out. So who knows?

All I know is, when you do parlay yourself, it's a blast to see how your investment can grow in a short time. Keep cool, learn, and have fun.

LOW BALLING CAN GET GOOD DEALS

You may have an opportunity to be involved in certain silent bids. Occasionally, some thrift stores have an area where some of their better donations and antiques are displayed and left for bidders to determine the selling price. After a week or so, the bids are reviewed and the winning bidder is notified. Sometimes you can get a pretty good deal, especially if your item hasn't had any other bidders. But how do you know? You can't. You have to guess. Is the item you're after something that many people seek? Is the store in a mainstream high traffic area where many collectors have a chance to visit? Historically, have you lost bids to similar items in that store?

Sometimes there are also some real bad shoppers who either don't know their products or just like to pay too much, and their bid causes them to over pay. You might try and do some low-balling, which is to bid much lower than the market price. Yes, your chances are less than ever to win the bid, but your chance to win a better profit is much greater. If there are many different items you bid on in a given time, you do have a good chance in getting something, even with low-ball bids.

This is difficult if you really hope you will have the winning bid, but, you may be willing to do so to get a good price.

Let's say you see an antique in the store that has a restored value of $1,000. This value increases when you clean, repair, and restore it. Its value "as found" is $400; that is, if you get it, you know a dealer or collector might pay you $400. You could easily bid $200 or even $250 for the item and feel pretty good about it, right? Or you could low-ball the bid and hope to get it for $100 or $150. Oh, but you might not get it, right?

Let's see how we would feel at certain prices on our $400/$1,000 item:

If you pay $250, it's okay.

If you pay $200, it's better.

If you pay $175, it's really good.

If you pay $150, it's great!

If you pay $100, it's fantastic!

If you pay $50, it's a steal!

If you pay $10, it's unbelievable and embarrassing.

What you are doing is buying a deal. You have to decide just what deal you wish to purchase. If you think about this chart before you make the bid, you end up with one of these deals if you win.

If you have found a way to remove emotion from the bidding, all the better. Sometimes we just really need to have something and bid too high, get stuck with it, tired of it, and have a hard time moving the item. This just frustrates us and ties up our dollars and we essentially bought that kind of a deal.

Sometimes a little studying before the bid and taking the time to write down pros and cons before we put down a price will help.

Ask some questions like:

How bad do I really want it? (Add or subtract $.)

Is it for my own personal collection? (Add $.)

Is it for resale for a profit? (Subtract $.)

Is it pre-sold? Do I have a buyer now with cash in hand? (Add $.)

Do I have the spare cash to buy this right now? (Remember, if you don't get it, you still have your money. You can always find a truly good deal at another time.) Also, make a list of the competitors that are likely to bid on it. Here's the final breakdown:

Value at list price is $1,000.

Street price is $800.

As found price is $400.

Highest I'd go is $250.

At $100, I'm sure to lose it.

The ideal price would be $150.

I'm going to bid $180 and I'd feel pretty good about the deal, and then live with the outcome. On small items, like $5-$10, don't sweat it, just go by your gut feeling and try to pick up a good deal by low-balling.

BEING LAST CAN HAVE BENEFITS

The assumption is that if you are the first person to a sale, you'll do well. If you can even be one of the lucky few who are invited to preview a sale before the public is invited, even better. Yes, you'll have the best selection. Yes, you'll have less competition. Yes, you'll have the best finds, deals, sleepers, etc.

The last person to a sale has benefits, too. Here's where you get the best price because now they just want to get rid of it. You also may get lucky and be there when they happen to find something tucked away and forgot to put in the sale. You can get lot prices on the leftovers. You might even get piles of stuff for free just for hauling it off. Stuff that was priced way too high, and the seller wasn't going to budge on the price, might go dirt-cheap at the end of the day. But then again, it might not be there, so don't plan on it; just recognize those end-of-the-day deals and finds when you see them.

TOOLS OF THE TRADE

It might be good to have a few tools available when you are out in the field picking to keep in your car:

- A good, bright L.E.D. flashlight. Flashlights are great, especially in a dark old place that has had old things hidden for years. It's good to have one for looking into old equipment, too.
- A good pocketknife is wonderful. One with a little but sturdy screwdriver is best, especially if the screwdriver blade is good for Phillips and flat-blade screws. My little Swiss one is nice. You might go a bit further and get one of those multi-tools that have everything from pliers to knives to bits coming out of everywhere.
- Cash, a checkbook, and coins for the phone, unless you use a cell phone, are a must.
- A tiny magnet might prove useful someday. You also might want to have a magnifying lens.
- Boxes and bags in the car might be handy, and a blanket to cover your car upholstery is needed sometimes.
- Here's a good reason for those little wash towelettes in the glove box—old stuff is dirty. Some of it is especially gross.

Have your little black book or a good smart phone with all of your contacts

This is a great way to display like items, such as these vintage canes. It not only keeps items neat, it makes it easier for pickers specializing in canes to sort through.

in it. All of the handy numbers of dealers and buyers is invaluable. Hopefully your phone has a great camera. You may need to send shots to people to check for more information, or even to give you offers on items that you can pre-sell. The phone should have a good Internet browser so you can research on the fly. There are several apps with barcode readers to help you price newer items. If you keep a want list, you might want this information available. Be prepared, scouters.

YOUR SHOPPING LIST

Create an antique picker's shopping list and write down your goals. Make a list of all the things you hope you will find as you are out picking. Once you have wants that are written, something magical happens in your subconscious: Your eyes and ears are programmed and piqued.

For example, I needed a box stapler to assemble boxes for shipping products on eBay. The stapler is one of those big units with handles that you crunch a large copper-colored staple to fasten heavy cardboard. I tried a few fastener places, and asked if they had a used one, because I was not about to pay $200 for a new one. I put it on my "shopping list." I was out one day and had a load of stuff I was shipping UPS, the reason I needed a stapler. I saw a pawnshop, which I do not go into regularly. I do enjoy the show *Pawn Stars*, however. In the back of my mind, I thought that they usually carry all sorts of tools, so I decided to see what they might have. Because I had it on my list and knew exactly what it looked like, within five minutes, I found my box stapler. It was $59. When talking about the stapler to the pawnshop owner, he said it was the only one he had ever seen and if I wanted it, I could have it for $10! "Oh, OK, sure!" I said.

Put *anything* you want on your written shopping list.

HELLO, FUTURE MILLIONAIRES!

A few years ago, way before *American Pickers*, *Pawn Stars*, and even *Antiques Roadshow*, I saw a special on TV about millionaires. There seemed to be a common thread among many of the millionaires they interviewed. They were millionaires not because they were lucky, but because they worked hard and they were *frugal* and *thrifty*. Before they were millionaires, they lived like they were rich because they had stuff like the rich, but did not pay a rich man's price for it. They would buy second-hand. They would buy items on sale. They looked for closeouts, and had great stuff they paid very little for. When you are living in the world of pickers, you are a millionaire in embryo. You find valuable items you pay very little for. Pickers enjoy finding things to resell and pickers find great deals on things they use, have, keep, and consume. **WARNING:** It will sort of change you and ruin and destroy you in a way. You will discover that you will have a difficult time paying retail or list price for anything ever again. I actually get kind of nauseous thinking I need to go to a regular store and buy anything that is especially expensive. I usually always shop three or four places like I am some sort of purchasing agent looking for the rock bottom price on something.

Let's go back to our millionaire comparison. If you want to be a millionaire, all you need to do is spend $500,000 on items at half price, $250,000 on items that are 75 percent off, or spend $100,000 on "ten cents on the dollar" products.

Picking for a profit is just the half of it. Picking for items for yourself and your family at a deep discount can be much better than getting a raise at work. You will improve your lifestyle and lift your standard of living. You can stretch and increase the value of your dollars. So much of the news is loaded with the decreasing value of the dollar. Here is a way to reverse that. Buying for pennies on the dollar is better than Wall Street.

An ammunitions table set up an at an antiques show. Do not put these types of items in your carry-on bag when flying!

YOU NEED TO HAVE MONEY

I recently got a phone call from someone asking if I still liked antiques. The caller said that a studio he works for had a problem with the city and had lost about one half of their real estate. They had to clean out the buildings and storage areas and attics of a collection that probably dated back a hundred years. He said there were WWI- and WWII-era collectibles, and local, original art just as old, and lots and lots of stuff. He said he was tight with the people and might be able to get me in with him the next night, a couple of days before the "rummage sale." He also said they didn't even have an idea of what the stuff was or its worth.

Problem was, I just paid bills and didn't have any money for antiques, but I went to a sneak preview of the rummage sale anyway. It was run by a non-profit organization, where people went to do crafts, learn art, and attend all kinds of classes. It had been a wonderful organization to have in our city for many years and people had donated all sorts of antiques and various items to them, probably for tax write-offs.

The first thing I saw was tons of old books, and a woman trying her hardest to look up books on Amazon, so they could price them for the sale, but she wouldn't get even close to Amazon prices. Then there was a large pile of dark-room equipment and old wooden box cameras.

They had in a back room tables set up with old donated actual pioneer-era clothing and had no idea what to do with it. There was old furniture, but while there, they said that an antiques dealer came in and bought lots of pieces. Wonder what they got? There were dolls, projectors, toys, a WWII field pump organ, and stuff everywhere. There was also original artwork.

I suggested they invite an estate sale dealer in to help them price it, but they said they did not have the time and besides, everything was pure profit to them, so they really did not care what they got for it.

I bought a box of old books, three old large format Kodak Wood cased cameras, a German camera lens, and a WWII 35MM aircraft bomb sight movie camera in its case with all the lenses. They were happy to see the stuff go and it was off to eBay to do some listing for me.

I went back the next day, too, and got two old projectors (pre-slide type) and one was a Victor Stereopticon. I also picked up some film holders for the antique Kodak cameras I got. I found an old Tour Ship jacket for Korea/Japan for the USS O'Bannon DD-450 Battleship. I found dozens of antique marionette and puppet heads that I thought might sell on eBay or keep as Halloween decorations. I also picked a few more antique books and a cool life-sized plaster casting of what looks like an actual human skull. It was a pretty good "picking for antiques" day and I had no real competition, other than a few other people they let in, too.

NEVER FALL IN LOVE... WITH YOUR INVENTORY

I learned from another wise man in the business this sage advice. "Never fall in love with your inventory." Know what you have and realize it's potential, but be a little aloof. You have got to not care about it. You may need to treat it like you are a mercenary. You may think your item is fantastic, you may think it's worth a gob of money. Sure, you bought it right. It was cheap. The item is worth a hundred times what you paid. Problem is, you may never get what it is worth, only what could be considered a fair offer. You are tempted to hold out for more. If you wait or negotiate too high, you will likely lose the sale and never get a chance to find a willing buyer again... ever!

Inside an industrial storage unit.

At a place I used to work, I had a cranky boss who had an old tired main-frame computer that they replaced. I'll just put some random numbers here, as it was a long time ago. They got the new computer and the computer salesman said, "We'll give you $5,000 for your old one, refurbish it, and sell to another company." The boss was angry and said, "I paid $50,000 for it, you are crazy, I'm holding on to it." The salesman came back in six months and said, "We'll give you $1,000 for it and I think we have a sale." The boss got real mad and pointed out the original offer was $5,000. They explained that was six months ago and that customer was gone. Six months later, the boss asked us to call the salesman and get the $1,000 for it. He didn't know who to sell it to. They said sorry, but in order to remove it and dispose of it properly, they would need to charge $250. He went ballistic. An employee finally gave him $25 to take it home for his teenage son to take apart and learn something about computers. Do not fall in love with stuff. Take the good profit, buy something else and make an additional profit, and repeat again, and again. This is what is called "the law of turnover." Turn over the money four or five times in a short while, and you'll make more dollars than you wanted in the first place for that original item.

I BUY STUFF AT AUCTIONS

I like certain types of auctions, particularly silent ones. We have a local company that holds occasional warehouse auctions this way. They might even have over 1,000 lots. You would think that a thousand lots would be too much to see, but it's not. The human mind is conditioned to be aware of everything in its immediate surroundings. Humans have used this ability forever. Early times it was a way of sustaining and protecting life. A human can walk into the forest and subconsciously see all of the tools and resources that are available nearby. This was used to find immediate defense and protection. It's the way to find food. It's the way soldiers can fight to stay alive. You will see in some movies, how the hero spots a way out, or discover a weapon in a split second, as they zoom in on it. So whether it's in a forest, a war, an urban environment, or out picking, it works. When I am searching for likely items at these auctions, I go in with an unwritten list in my head. I am constantly adding new wants. My experiences give me tools. I see potential profits as I walk around, and I find items to buy, and then sell. It works the same with every estate sale or yard sale, etc. I will find my stuff, you will find your stuff, and most of the time it will be completely different. I think I am the one who is lucky, smart, or blessed, and you will think those same thoughts as you pick up your different pieces.

Live auctions can be great, too. The problem is, unless you are disciplined, you can pay too much in a split second and end up with a terrible case of buyers regret. On the other hand, you might go away with an amazing deal everyone else missed. Sometimes auctioneers will let a few at first go really fast and cheap to get everyone excited. I do like auctions. They are great fun. I would recommend that you find all of the live auction companies in your local area and sign up for their emails. Always preview online and in person before the auction starts. Make your decisions before the fervor starts.

HOT ITEMS FOR ANTIQUES PICKERS

What is a hot item to find? My collectibles-picking list will be different than yours, and my list is different than my wife's list. I go for guy stuff, actually probably nerd or geek guy stuff. I like to pick for vintage technical items including old radios: regular, shortwave, "ham radios," even transistor and crystal radios, etc.; old LED pocket calculators, and LED watches; electron tubes of any kind; tube audio and stereo equipment; microphones; microscopes; mini tape recorders; weird or "futuristic" TVs and tape players; old cameras (Leica, Nikon, etc.); old technical engineering books; slide rules; scientific and test equipment; vintage electronic parts; telegraph and wireless items; vintage "pate de verre" glass objects; early advertising items for any items I pick; early computers; and space and robot toys.

These are items I am excited about. This is why I am a picker. Any early, heavy, "that's so cool" items. I do buy items like above and would welcome inquiries through the comments entry, if you have things to sell. I may be a little hesitant, based on shipping expense, but hey, contact me; I could also advertise it here if I don't want to buy it.

I like this stuff because I was in the electronic component distribution business for many years and this created nostalgia in me for items in my field. I started slow as a picker, thinking I was just lucky in finding good stuff. Then the more I researched and read about stuff in magazines, I really went crazy. If you have been in the medical field, you may collect old doctor's bags and tools. If you are into automotive collectibles, it's probably because you repair cars, etc. You are welcome to contact me at www.pickersbible.com, if you have some stuff I like.

TIME TRAVEL IN A THRIFT STORE AND AN ANTIQUES SHOP

I found a brand new in box iPad 3 in a thrift store. It was only $15. This was not recent, but this will be in a few short years I'm sure.

The calculators we used to have to pay $100s for are now a couple of dollars. Expensive video game consoles, computers, and bestseller books are pennies on the dollar. But what goes around comes around. Those very first calculators may now only be $2 in the thrift store, but could be again tens or even hundreds of dollars to collectors. It's all time travel. I remember when the Texas Instruments representative came into our electronic store many years ago with their first prototype pocket LED calculator. It was encased in clear Plexiglas so you could see the large integrated circuit they made and the TIXL series LED display. I'd pay a bunch for one of those prototypes for my collection.

A thrift store is especially a time travel machine. You can go to several different dates, back in time, and see what was around. An antiques store is a little more specialized, as it has just the more interesting and valuable items throughout time. The thrift store has all the other junk, too. They smell different, too, but the smells are the same no matter where you go. The thrift store has additional "old humans" mustiness. Old bookstores have old paper mustiness, altogether different. Antiques stores have dusty mustiness smells. And the best is old radio collections they have the antiques store's dusty musty and additional Bakelite and phenolic smell mixed in. I especially like, in this order: old radio smell, bookstores, antiques store smell. I don't care for thrift store smell it makes me want to wash my hands a lot. If you are an avid picker, what is your favorite smell?

PICKER'S SECRET: OTHER WAYS TO FIND GOLD

Because I am a picker, I not only look for antique stuff, I look for *valuable* stuff. I am interested in the technical side of junk. I love old radios, electronics, and industrial surplus, and I make a lot of money buying and selling all kinds of stuff.

One thing I have been doing is collecting e-waste. Electronic waste has the potential of being a gold mine for you. There is quite a bit of gold plating, especially on the old stuff (after tubes, and just as transistors and early computers came on). I have even written an eBook on the subject, *E-Waste Gold!*, that can be bought on amazon.com. If you have any questions or suggestions on the subject of reclaiming gold and silver, platinum, and palladium, please let me know. I just had about 800 pounds of the stuff refined, and got a real nice settlement.

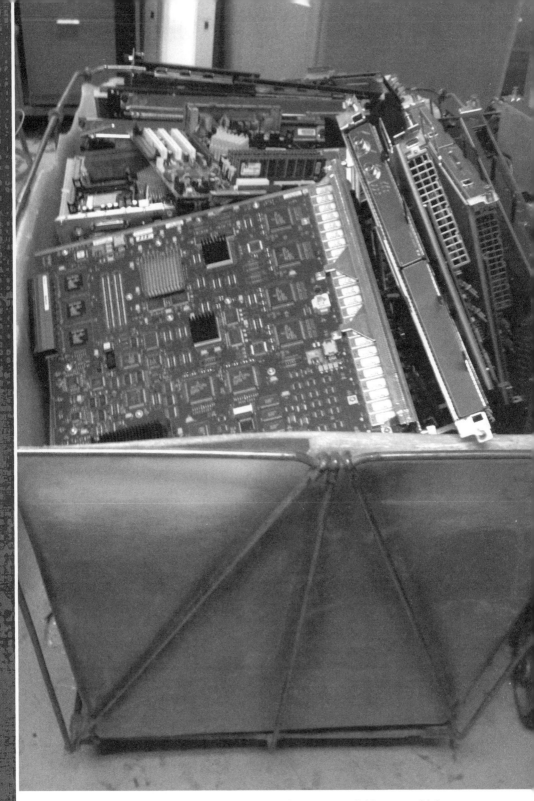

Industrial picking is hot right now and electronic scrap can yield a pretty high gold value.

COULD HAVE, SHOULD HAVE, WOULD HAVE ... IF ONLY!

I have regrets often in this business. It's usually after a "live" auction. Like the one I went to recently. I went to the sale preview on two different days and found all of the items I thought I'd want. I marked them on the auction lot list. I researched values online through Google, eBay, Amazon, etc. I thought I was pretty ready. I even had money in the bank! Right off, I won an item and then lost an item. Yeah, I think I would have bid higher on the one I lost, but they had more coming up. Problem is, the first one was the best, and all of the rest went for higher prices. I was still okay, but then I bought an item I had not even seen on the preview inspection, which was another regret. I paid too much. No one else bid, so that must have meant something. Then I felt pretty good, as I won a couple of additional items on my list, one of which I got for a lot less than I would have. I was going to go as high as $200 on a special tool and got it for $50! Then it happened: One of the items I wanted came up and feeling I was lucky on the others, as the price started increasing, I backed out. It went for $150. Looking back, it was something I really did want and would have gone as high as $350. The problem was this: I had not decided a top price beforehand. The auctioneer went fast, I saw it was going up fast, and I backed down. I lost. Today, even though I really won some nice items, I keep sulking and moaning about this one that got away.

For live auctions, you need to decide in advance what the highest price is that you will pay for each item. When is it no longer a good deal to you? If you lose it and it's not a good deal, and the other person paid way too much, you won't be left with regrets. If you ask, "If I lose this item and don't want to feel bad the next day, it's because I am willing to pay $_____ for it."

The auctioneer is making money from exciting the crowd. He is speaking fast to sell lots of "lots." He is speaking fast to keep you from having time to think. People will bid because of pride "so the other guy" won't be able to get it.

Your decision on how much you are going to spend per each lot, as an individual item, is most important. Your next decision is how much total you are going to spend, based on your financial situation at the time.

I have a request. Please write to me at pickersbible.com and let me know about your wins and regrets at live auctions. Also, do you have any "tips" you can give me before I go to the next auction? For example, is it better sitting in the front or the back of the room? Side or center? Does it matter how you dress if you dress nice, does it intimidate the competition, thinking you have more money? What other kinds of tips do you have? I'd like to do better next time.

THIS MIGHT BE WHY I LIKE ANTIQUES AND PICKING

I really suppose it was all instilled in me from my dear mother. I remember her showing me things when I was just a young child that were important to her. She also seemed to want to find old classic collectibles and save them for us. Once in a while, she would pull out an old book and say, "Maybe I should see if I could sell this ..." I'd always cringe and say, "No, it's an antique, you should hang on to it." I really think now that she was trying to make me learn that these historical things are important. She saw something in my care and concern for vintage items and tried to cultivate it.

I should have guessed it was her that secretly sent me a subscription to *Christies Auction Catalog*. I thought somehow they made a mistake and sent them to me or somehow I must have signed up for something and now received the catalogs for free. They came for several years. I did pour over them, seeing amazing and valuable items in their pages. I even mentioned items I had seen to mom several times. She stayed cool and never let on she was the provider of the subscription.

I would drag home stuff that I felt was important from thrift stores, from junk, from grandparent's homes, etc. She seemed to encourage it. She would take pride in my finds. She loved old things, too. She was an amazing and smart woman. Thanks Mom!

TAILGATING AT ESTATE SALES

I saw something interesting when at an estate sale recently. There was a person who was parked out in front of the yard selling items. He had his back door opened and on the back seat was about eight or more handguns, all priced, ready to sell to people coming to the sale. I wonder about what he was selling, of course, but I thought it was a brilliant idea to follow someone else's ad, which will bring many individuals, and tailgate, selling your own stuff. I'd really like to see this expand and have it be a regular occurrence at sales: people selling collectibles, antiques, or whatever. Mini flea markets while you are out hunting.

I posted about this on my blog and a reader said: *You're kidding, right? Selling handguns from the backseat. I can't think of a better way to find a new career WORKING IN JAIL! First off you CAN NEVER EVER sell firearms in any state out of the back of your car. Secondly, even if you are selling other merchandise, you risk getting a ticket at the very least if you don't have a "peddler's license" in many jurisdictions; you can't be sure whoever is run-*

ning the sale is not going to be happy and probably will call the local police if they find out about you. There is also a question of loitering. I could go on and on but bottom line: DUMB IDEA!

My response: I did not say I approve of selling the guns this way, but if you do a search, it is entirely legal in most states to sell guns at yard sales and the like. I think the "tailgating" idea could be interesting in selling antiques and collectibles, etc., piggybacking onto a larger, say, neighborhood yard sale event, because hey, why not!

WHAT A DUMMY I HAVE BEEN

I am not only a "live picker," that is, picking at estate and garage sales, etc., but I am a "virtual picker." I buy great deals from eBay and other online sources and then turn around and sell them for the actual value. I'm not going to tell you what I got recently, but it cost me $55 and is actually worth $950. I suppose this is a form of eBay arbitrage! It works all the time.

But I am here to admit, I have been dumb. I'm sure some of you are just as dumb, too.

I have been a pretty big user, until now, of the "eBay Watch List." It's been part of the fun of buying stuff cheap and selling high. Sometimes my competition is pretty fierce, and my competition has, in fact, been caused *by me*!

eBay advertises to other buyers, especially ones who are looking for similar items I have been watching, that I am watching what they want. For example: Let's say for kicks that I am watching for a Pet Rock. I find a cool one for $.99 and I really really want it. I used to click as soon as I could to add it to my watch list. Now, when my competition is looking for a Pet Rock, and somehow missed the one I picked to watch, it gets shown "See what others are watching" and shows my item because it's on my stupid watch list. Dang! What a dummy I've been.

It would be better to just quietly save my searched item in a file or an email. Or, if you use a sniping service like esnipe.com, you can place your bid now, but it will not show up anywhere on eBay until the last second. You can still get reminders through esnipe, etc.

I now use my eBay watch list just for pricing stuff or reminders, etc. Everything of real value is now hidden from others.

This dealer specializes in Mid-Century kitchen and Art Deco groupings.

Chapter 6

....

Be the
Better Picker

By now you may have tried a few of the ideas and techniques discussed while you've been picking for stuff. You also have many of your own secrets that have proven helpful. You have made money and found all kinds of prizes and treasures. The problem is still the other pickers out there.

You have met all kinds of people: pickers, dealers, charlatans, and all sorts of wheeler-dealers. Some people are clever and shrewd, some are smart. There are successful ones and the others who don't get it. You'll find the ones you can trust and some who are out-and-out crooks. Now what?

The first hint is: *learn*. Watch, listen, find out how and why people do things, and you'll come out on top. As you learn how a colleague picker scooped you on a deal, you get better. No, you didn't get the items, nor did you make the profit, but now you are armed with a bit more knowledge and experience. This also goes especially for bad deals that others make. You learn without losing money.

Why do some pickers do better than others? It starts with the passion they have for the profession; the motivation to learn all they can about the antiques and collectibles they are interested in picking; and the curiosity to ask questions to other pickers, dealers, collectors, store owners, and everyone else they meet so that they can grow and be successful.

SET REALISTIC AND MANAGEABLE GOALS

Goal setting works in any line of work or venture. As you study and gain likes, tastes, and wants, don't be afraid to set some goals. You may want to find the best or the finest doohickey ever made. You might never find it, but in looking for it may find something almost as neat or even much better.

Get a good book on goal setting; even better, find one when you're out picking and follow the advice for setting and accomplishing goals.

Realize this: You really can have absolutely anything you really want. Just make sure you have good wants.

A STOREFRONT PUTS YOU IN FRONT

Those who have a storefront always have an advantage over others, as there are constantly people bringing items to them. This is a form of advertising: People see your place and they might have something like they saw in your display and either bring something similar in to unload or spread the word to others who have things to sell. It brings a lot of stuff on the market that would never have surfaced normally. This is in addition to pickers who bring these dealers many items. I know of a company that has had a storefront selling surplus electronics for years. The owner recently retired after about 50 years, and never did do much advertising. People just knew he was there, through word of mouth, and bought from him or sold to him. He made a good living from people just walking in the front door. This business model can work in all sorts of fields. Child-related and clothes-related businesses buy and sell used items all the time. Office supplies and other companies buy and sell.

SCORING FREEBIES

After you get involved in a specialty, you might find that occasionally people you know or meet will give you stuff for free. You might have relatives or neighbors call you and tell you to come over because they have something for you. I know a collector who was fortunate enough to get his antique television collection featured on a television program a few years back. He had many people call, asking him to just come on over and pick up vintage televisions from their garages and basements.

One time I received a call from someone who picked up one of my cards at a show and said he had some stuff similar to what I was collecting and selling. He filled up my car trunk with books and classic collectible items. This is a good reason to list all of your interests on your business cards because you never know where or when that card may end up.

You might not be able to get free exposure on television, but if you approach your local library and ask if you can put a display out on the items you collect, I'm sure you'll have people coming from all directions. Many libraries have beautiful locked display cases set up for purposes just like this.

DRUM UP YOUR OWN HYPE

The best way to get the market going on your items is to start or join in on the hype. By hype, I mean the speeches at symposiums, the articles written in newsletters, the talks and show and tell at club meetings, etc. One of the latest and best ways to do this is to start an interest group through an online service, meetup.com, which is a great way to find other people with like interests. You can start it with you alone and start inviting others. The online promotion through the searches and the service will find others to join for you. Once you have the people, then marketing and ultimately "commerce" of some sort can be involved. Hype might sound negative, but what I describe here is nothing more than building knowledge, which begets interest and appreciation. This then creates value, which makes demand and creates sales. As others learn of the finer points of something antique, or unique, they really start to bond with it.

Christie's and Sotheby's publish some of the most magnificent catalogs with absolutely gorgeous full-color photography. They write wonderful articles on the history and importance of the products they will be selling. The catalogs are instructive and tell you why you need to have an item by creating interest. They include stories of influential collectors in the catalog to add value.

You might look at some ways to start some action in your particular field of interest in your local area. It will pay off. You will create new collectors. You'll see new stuff comes from all sorts of new sources you didn't even know about. You can either find treasures in trash, or with hype, you can create new treasures from trash.

Some collectibles, especially those newly emerging or pre-collectibles, need lots of hype to gather and sustain interest. Those pushing these newer products deemed collectible use much publicity and advertising to keep interest going.

WAYS TO CREATE HYPE AND EXCITEMENT AROUND ITEMS

- Starting a club or meetup with meetings, a newsletter, emails, etc.
- Having a special showing, inviting certain collectors.
- Advertising a special swap meet.
- Having an auction.
- Publishing a newsletter.
- Becoming an authority by writing a new book on your emerging collectible.
- Doing a public interest TV spot or local newspaper article on your specialty. The more obscure or esoteric it is, the better chance you'll get a reporter's attention.
- Placing an intriguing ad in the classifieds that will bring other collectors to you for you to sell to or buy from.
- Inspiring your friends to get into the field.
- Partnering with someone with similar interests.
- Cornering the market on something you feel will be hot. (Be careful!)
- Putting a display in a mall or public library.
- Renting part of your collection as a display or mini museum somewhere.
- Having a special display of items for sale in an antiques showcase mall.
- Searching on the internet for others with the same new interest.
- Renting, selling, or leasing your collection as movie props.
- Starting a blog, feature in Facebook, Pinterest, Tweet new finds, etc.
- Becoming a regular author for national magazines.

For you to promote and generate lots of interest, you need to collect the items. You then need to inspire others to collect them. You need to point out your likes and descriptions and define classic features. You need to encourage people who collect stuff like you find because it gets people to establish new wants and it increases values and gives prices meaning.

Sometime, just watch how a good dealer who runs an antiques mall works. If some customer asks questions or makes conversation on a particular item in the store, he sells it based upon his own interest and affection for the item. He hypes it up, the enthusiasm is infectious, and the customer goes home excited about the purchase.

Hype is actually a form of advertising. It fans the fire, it plays with pride and for a moment, magnifies obsession. After all, the process of obtaining an item is always much more pleasurable than actually having it. When you sell an item or even hint there is competition, it can raise the fervor, as several collectors will fight for the same item.

A HELPFUL TIP FOR FINDING STUFF

I spoke to a collector who collects a unique, expensive item that is usually hard to find, but his method for finding it can work for all sorts of items. Steve would get in his car while on vacation and target certain rural areas in his state or others nearby. He would find small town libraries, grocery stores, gas stations, and Laundromats—any place that might have a bulletin board. He'd tack up either a business card or a small poster that said what he wanted. His little signs were successful. He was finding his treasures in all kinds of strange places. He would then drive to farms and go to barns, garages, old closed buildings, and other places and obtain some remarkable deals.

LISTENING BETWEEN THE LINES

You really need to listen. One time at a place I worked, I overheard a fellow employee talking to someone about his parents moving and selling some stuff. It must have registered in my mind a few days later and I asked him if his parents were still moving. He said they were already gone. I asked what they did with all of their old stuff and he said much went to second-hand donations, some was sold, etc. We talked about what they had, including vintage tube audio equipment, Klipsch speakers, turntables, and other valuable collectibles. I missed out by not really listening. This was a "lead" and you need to follow-up on leads.

Another time I happened to be talking to a fellow employee about collecting radios, and when the stock boy walked by and heard some of the conversation, he said if I liked old radio stuff, he'd bring in something for me. He brought in an old Vibroplex "bug" telegraph key his grandfather used while working on the railroad and sold it to me for $20. I found out much later that this key was so old, it was the first generation that Vibroplex made and probably a prototype. I showed it to an expert, who said it must be a prototype because this did not have the serial number they always put on their devices. It was a wonderful find, and the chances happening when I got it were one in a million.

HAVE A GOOD BUSINESS CARD

Advertising pays. You might not have a storefront to hang a sign outside, but you can do other things to announce you are in business, such as making an attention-getting business card and tell what kind of stuff you pick for. Have them printed professionally—the finer your card looks and feels, the more respect it brings.

Hand out the cards and leave them at all the sales you visit and you will get calls and referrals. If you sell at a show or swap meet, put a stack out for people to pick up. Give to friends, collectors, dealers, and antiques stores everywhere.

Here's an example of what the card could say:
Always looking for: Old Furniture
Old Watches, Old Fountain Pens, Old Jewelry
Garage sale nut!
(Your name)
Phone: 111-111-1111; email: xxx@xxx.com
Buy & Sell • Trade & Swap

If you do shows, make up a noticeable and unique sign on what you are looking for. Put the cards just below the sign. You can't imagine how much business this brings. You'll get stuff brought right over to you. Keep it simple:

WANTED: OLD WATCHES
I collect old watches. Please take a card.

A grouping of silver and fabric items at an antiques show.

DON'T BECOME ATTACHED

Warning: Sentimental thinking can get you in trouble, whether you are buying or selling. If you are at an estate sale and someone tries to justify an obviously way too high price because it's been in the family for years, it is just sentimentality. Sentimentality needs to go out of the window as soon as an item is up for sale. There is no value or profit justified by sentimentality. Historical items owned by important and famous individuals are a different story if you can prove or document the ownership, which is called "provenance."

One time I responded to a classified ad where an old man wanted to sell his favorite radio. When I asked what it was and how much he wanted, he gave me an unbelievably high price. He said it was his pride and joy. Sorry, but I can't buy your memories along with it.

KEEP OR SELL? TAKE THE MONEY

If you are a purely mercenary picker and have no problem selling every item you come across, you won't have a problem with this topic. What if you are a collector, too, and really like a whole lot of the stuff you find? Here's a rationalization exercise for you to work through when this problem comes up, and I guarantee you'll be faced with this, since there is an awful lot of cool stuff out there that you'll be tempted to hold onto.

When you need to decide whether to sell an item or keep it, answering a few of these questions will help you know what to do:

- The easy question: Would you rather have the money or the item? First think of the cash amount, now think of the item—and then decide. (Could you afford to buy it for what it is worth?)
- If the dollars you received were then traded for the equivalent in silver or gold coins, how big would the stack be? Now think if the silver or gold is better than the item.
- Is the item absolutely rare and irreplaceable? Is it likely to show up again in a few months? Is it the best quality one you have ever seen?
- If you have this item and many other items you could move and liquidate, could you get one better item you'd really rather have?
- Are you investing in this item, hoping to gain a return at a later date? Can you realistically predict whether it is likely to appreciate or depreciate?
- Could you do better on a trade than you could cash it out?
- Do you really use, study, or even enjoy and appreciate it, or is it just another conquest?
- Are you getting tired of it?
- Do you have a sale for it?
- Is that sale likely to go away?

PICK ITEMS YOU CAN FLIP FAST

If you can grasp the importance of turn over, you will make more money. It's almost like understanding the law of saving money. If you do, you will have more money. Measuring turn over is a way to see how your dollars make more dollars.

Sitting with too many dollars tied up in wonderful, rare, and beautiful antiques can kill your operation. This is why various companies will have a sale. They understand they need to get the money out of the inventory. This will help them use the dollars to make more dollars. They will have closeout sales or mark down merchandise to get the dollars out quickly. They realize it might be better to take a bath on the slow moving or dead stock, so they liquidate or convert it to cash. They use this new cash to buy faster-moving items. This gives them profit.

In a nutshell, if you take $100 you invest in inventory and sell the item for $150, you made a $50 profit. If you do that four times a year, you turned that

$100 four times, netting you $200 in profit. If you had a faster-moving item that you could turn over ten times, you would net $500 in profit.

Turn over is the secret to profit. Margin or mark-up only tells you part of the story: How much you made on one transaction. Here's another example: I buy an item for $10 and sell it for $1,000. This sounds like a sweet deal, doesn't it? But if I have 200 more of those $10 items in stock sitting and not selling, I have still not made any profit (200 x $10 = $2,000). I made back $1,000, but I still have $1,000 of my money tied up. Going the other extreme, if I sell them quickly for $50 each, much less than their $1,000 list price (200 x $50 = $10,000). On my original $2,000 cost, I made $8,000 profit.

You can develop a turnover ratio and not only make more profit but gain happy customers, too. You will have more variety and interesting things to buy.

Figuring a turnover ratio is comparing your sales to the value of the inventory. To figure inventory turns on your overall business, use the following formula:

Beginning Inventory **plus** Purchases **minus** Ending Inventory **divided by** Average Inventory **equals** Turns.

(Average Inventory **equals** Beginning Inventory **plus** Ending Inventory **divided by** 2.)

IF BETTER SERVICE MEANS HIGHER INCOMES

Examples	A	B	C
Beginning Inventory	$2,000	$1,000	$1,000
+ Purchases	$1,000	$1,000	$5,000
- Ending Inventory	$1,000	$1,000	$1,000
/ Average Inventory	$1,500	$1,000	$1,000
= Turns	1.333	1	5
	(Poor)	(Poor)	(Good)

So when we look at example A above, we see that our beginning inventory is $2,000, we purchased $1,000, and at the end of the year we still had $1,000 in inventory, giving us an average inventory of $1,500. This gave us a turnover ratio on our investment of $1,000 of 1.33, which was pretty poor. You'll also notice that nothing was mentioned about how much profit margin I made. You might have any range of profit margin.

It is agreed that the higher the margin, the better. But more importantly, your money is re-invested and at work for you. So if I make 50 percent GP on a $50 item, but can sell it twelve times in that same year, it nets me $180. If I take the same item, but sell it more times during the year, it gets me more profit that I can save, spend, or re-invest. As long as I turnover my invested dollars, I'm making money. If I hoard, I lose money. If I buy stuff that doesn't sell, I lose money. Always buy stuff that moves quickly and then sell it.

What I really like is when I find an item and sell it on the same day. Talk about a quick turnover. I was at a swap meet once where, out of the corner of my eye, I saw an item come in on a truck with several other items that I quickly recognized. I asked how much and was told $75. I said "sold" and asked him to wheel it over to my space. In about an hour, I re-sold the piece for $300. After thinking about it, I never even touched it with my hands.

This also works for people who have a rented showcase in an antiques mall. You may see an item in another dealer's case and recognize its potential. You see that there is a profit in the item because the other dealer has it priced too low. Just buy it, mark it up, and place it in your case. There is risk in this, but a quick-flip profit is possible.

KEEP YOUR INVENTORY FLUID

I have some friends who buy much of the same type of stuff as I do, and I sell or trade many items with them. But one problem I see them struggle with is that they keep it all. One has a house with items everywhere and also a garage with loads of items packed to the ceiling. He used to pay good money to rent a storage unit until he wised up and built his own storage shed—but now that is full. The other just has a storage shed he rents because he lives in an apartment. I have a shop I built adjoining my house. Yes, it is full, but I move a lot of items. The inventory changes and turns over. My personal collection evolves depending on what I want to collect at a particular time.

What happens is that I learn, study new items, new technologies, and different histories and trends in items I collect. I enjoy the items, upgrade the things I eventually keep, and most importantly, I profit.

Some people pile it up, though, and never see anything, and refuse to sell anything because they want to keep it.

I was in an estate once where the man had no basement, just a four-foot crawl space. Over the years, he piled his treasures, packing every square foot of the space. His poor daughter had to clean it all out after he died. He put it all back there, but never saw or enjoyed it again—but it was *his*. To clean out the house after his death, she needed to rent a large commercial dumpster and actually filled it three times. There were things back in the crawl space from the 1950s that had never seen the light of day since he dragged them back there.

What happens is by keeping it all, you don't have the cash to be involved in the good deals that come up and eventually, you start to avoid even looking at deals when you hear about them.

But too many forget that having an item is not nearly as enjoyable as pursuing and obtaining the item. Then there is the joy in selling it for a profit. Someone told me once that the best two days in your life is the day you buy a boat, and the day you sell it. I truly believe if you climb a little bit and then set your sights a little further, you will get much more satisfaction. This is one of the major benefits of a fluid collection: You absolutely enjoy it more and by keeping it fluid, you end up with better items and are in control of your wants.

You've got to sell, upgrade, give away, study, donate, throw away, buy, trade, etc. or there is no profit.

If you like certain things, by all means, "Keep the best and trade off the rest." After all, you can't keep it all. You can't get it all, either. If you just buy an item and see it once and put it in a box, yes, it is yours, but you enjoy it very little and it will eventually be forgotten.

Why are we discussing this? What good does it do? First of all, I'm not trying to make you feel guilty—if in fact, you are guilty. If you recognize some of this in you, you will also see it in others you work with. You'll be a better picker if you know how it works.

Estates are filled with stuff that people bought or got and put away after seeing it once. If you display, fix, restore, use, clean, photograph, study, or document it, this will add value to it. If you trade and sell it, you enjoy the profits from it. It is exactly the same as a dividend from your investments.

If you hoard it all away, hoping or waiting for something, you lose interest, you lose profit, and you lose track of it. It gets forgotten. On one hand, thank goodness others do pile it up. This means there will be a constant supply for all of us. We get to search through all of their stuff and find goodies. On the other hand, be careful yourself.

So remember, you will find some stuff that is rare and irreplaceable and dear to your heart. Note this. Most every deal I do includes rare, hard-to-find, classic, and difficult to replace finds. This is exactly why we do it.

It's okay to have stuff, hold it, and do things with it. It is proper to keep it for a while, especially if it is an investment item that is likely to increase in value.

I think it's probably much easier for me to find, buy, and make good deals getting stuff than for me to sell the stuff. It's not that I am a poor salesman; it's just that I really hang onto the really neat stuff. But when I start converting

A nice, clean storage unit with three floors of indoor climate-controlled storage lockers.

it to cash, I find that is pretty neat, too. There is a lot more out there than you think. If you turn it over and make wise decisions buying, you'll be wealthy in no time. This is possible only if you reinvest the dollars in new good finds.

IT'S NOT A HOARDING CONTEST

New collectors and pickers may contract a hoarding fever. If you see this in yourself, think about these things:

1. You might start out in this field thinking you are too late and all of the good stuff is gone, so you go after anything and any quantity.
2. You seem to buy anything, in any kind of condition. You might buy at high prices and feel you're getting good deals because it will be worth more someday.
3. You always run out of money.
4. You run out of room fast.
5. You keep branching out into different fields having difficulty remembering

what you want in the first place, etc.

6. It gets difficult to let go of stuff because you seem to want it all. Parts and pieces and incomplete sets are valuable to you because you never know when you "might need these things."

7. You hang onto things because you think it will be difficult to ever find one of them again, they are too rare, or hard to replace, but there is hope!
   - You need to let go—sell something.
   - Be somewhat mercenary.
     A. Cash always improves if your goal is to turn over your money.
     B. If you are a collector and you sell stuff regularly, your collection will get better and better with fewer and fewer pieces as you improve and sell off. Your focus improves.
     C. Every time you sell an item, you gain contacts. Some valuable contacts are made through buying and selling.
     D. Your growth, knowledge, and experience blossoms. Yes, you will make bad decisions, lose good deals, and sell irreplaceable goods, but you'll find and keep even more rare pieces, make and find even better deals.
     E. Overall you'll have better stuff, enjoy it more, and have the cash when you need it for those good deals, which will come.
   - You need to specialize. You may want to let a few good deals slide by, unless you have a ready buyer for the goods. If you are not entirely familiar with the product, you can also be stuck.
   - "As long as you keep kicking yourself in the butt and patting yourself on the back, you'll keep moving forward."
   - You need to realize the education you receive is valuable, whether it's been a profitable good deal or a disaster. This way you are always on top.

Your cash flow is extremely important. If you don't have ready cash, you are effectively stopped. You don't have funds to buy in on new deals. You don't grow. The other guy gets in there and you lose out.

You need to keep this venture self-funding—that is, going ahead on its own money, without investing more from household funds or from debt.

Cash is like the air you breathe. If you run out of cash, you can't pay your vendors, and then your debt increases. You can't buy new stuff to sell. You also have more worry and stress which decreases motivation—then you make bad decisions.

You can have lots of great inventory and the best deals come your way. You can be the best picker in the field, but if you run out of air to breathe, you die anyway.

You need to make a balanced activity of buying and selling and trading constantly. By selling, I mean selling and getting paid for it.

So make some plans and watch your cash flow. Use the above list, and come up with more that might be unique to your business or area. Use it to inspire you with ideas of how to turn over your inventory.

ADOPT AN EXPECTANT AND POSITIVE ATTITUDE

I guess it has to do with creating new horizons. I tried to sell a rather expensive item I had recently obtained. It was taking up quite a bit of room, and it needed to find a place to go. I tried finding someone local at first, but ended up selling the item out of state. I also ended up with lots more than the sale. One person I contacted locally, someone I haven't needed to call for many years, opened up a bigger world because of things he is now into. True, he didn't buy the item from me, but many other deals and potential deals are happening. I am so glad I called. More profit will be made from this dead end than would have been made from the original item he didn't buy from me. This is how you can get many more valuable contacts.

You have a focus when you start to call around because you are asking about, searching for, and finding things. Because of your reason to call someone, it opens up a variety of possibilities, so be on the lookout for them. As you approach new opportunities with an expectant and positive attitude, you will always accomplish more.

CONSIDER WHOLESALE

You can spend lots of time, money, and effort in trying to get top dollar for each and every item you find—or you can wholesale it.

If you decide to sell and want to lot it out, don't feel bad if you don't get full-bore retail for it. After all, you may not have wanted to do everything on our value-added list to get retail.

Yes, it is difficult to sell an item for $40 when you know the person you sell it to will in turn sell it for $100. As a seller, if you have an opportunity to turn your money over quickly and have the cash to keep growing, it really does not matter.

PRICES AND VALUE OF VINTAGE STUFF

The original price of an item currently made is actually an illusion. Value can be deceptive. The manufacturer has established and created a market for

IDEAS FOR SELLING

By now you are good at finding lots of stuff, but now what do you do with it? How do you make a profit and turn it into cash? Here are a few ideas:

1. Wholesale it to dealers. Establish lots of good picker/dealer relationships.
2. Sell it directly to other local collectors.
3. Put it in a booth or showcase in an antiques mall.
4. Sell it at a swap meet or flea market.
5. Open up a store.
6. Go to a show specializing in your topic.
7. Advertise nationally and sell it mail order.
8. Put it on the eBay.
9. Contact a museum.
10. Place a classified ad in your local paper.
11. Swap it for faster-moving merchandise.
12. Keep some of it.
13. Put notes on bulletin boards around town.
14. Tell friends (get others to start collecting it, too).
15. Have a yard sale.
16. Contact people in your directory who specialize in the product.
17. Find other pickers for the items.
18. Make a mailing.
19. Go to a club meeting, announce what you have, or put an ad in their newsletter.
20. Have an auction, or consign it to an auction company for a fee.
21. Take some of it with you as you travel and contact others in that area.
22. Donate it to a non-profit, and receive a receipt for your donation.

something and they are entitled to get that price based on their design, their marketing, and their work. Its real value may be entirely different. Collector's items are collectible based upon similar illusions, "somebody wrote about it in an article" or "this guy I know has one of every type made" or "the price guide says..." You can remember that price illusions are fleeting when negotiating to obtain something. "Just because some price guide says $$$, I buy them all the time for $$ or even $..."

BE HAPPY WHEN YOU DON'T FIND ANYTHING

There's an interesting term, "getting skunked." If you go out one day looking for great deals and end up with next to nothing, it's time to celebrate. Be happy; in fact, get excited!

Now wait a minute, you say. I thought that this was all about finding trea-

BENEFITS OF WHOLESALING

1. You get cash in hand to buy more stuff. Cash flow justifies a business, whether it is a hobby business or a full-time business.
2. You just might buy (wholesale) items with that cash that propel you further into profit.
3. You might need the cash right now.
4. This may have been stock you have had in your inventory for a long time, not moving.
5. You may never find the right clientele to sell it for top dollar.
6. You might be tired of the item.
7. Sometimes, the buyer just really wants it.
8. You might be wishing to gain a favor with the buyer.
9. You might need the room.
10. You may have bought it for next to nothing so it's all profit.
11. Convert it in your mind into the next stuff you'll get, whether it is cash, gold, antiques, or debt relief. Which would you rather have? Wholesale it and move on.

sures and goodies. Now you say to be happy when we're not finding good stuff? Exactly. We all have bad days; in fact, lots of them. You may have to run for days or even weeks with barely enough to fill half of your trunk with just so-so stuff. Be prepared for those dry spells. Realize this major point: the more bad days out picking, the closer you are to your next big find. It's just like the door-to-door vacuum salesman. He would almost shout for joy every time he got a door slammed in his face because he knew he was literally one door closer to the person who would buy something from him. So when you come out empty handed, grin.

BUT KEEP BUYING TO KEEP YOUR BUSINESS GROWING

You not only need to keep selling, but you need to balance it out with buying. Unless a body keeps eating and consuming, it dies. Unless you keep buying continually and moving your inventory, your business dies.

If you don't keep finding new and interesting items, you're not growing. If you keep buying but not selling, your business gets constipated. If you neither buy, nor sell, your network dries up and you lose touch from the market, and then you lose interest and knowledge. You have to buy and sell, trade, read, learn, discover, and meet new people on a consistent basis.

I wanted to buy an estate I found a while back, but didn't have the ready cash to do so, so I advertised a lot of books I had previously bought for a reasonable price, between a quarter to $1 a piece. I ended up selling a portion of them, about 200 books, for a total of $3,000.

This was a healthy profit margin for me, but the dealer I sold them to made a much greater profit. I can't complain, though, because I needed the cash. The cash was to purchase another estate, which, in turn, I sold for a profit. This was my springboard. Sometimes you have to take a little loss turning your inventory over to realize a better net profit.

SCORING FINDERS' FEES AND FAVORS

After you get some good contacts and a network built up, you'll have certain individuals you know who specialize in various items. In your searches, you're bound to find some items that are highly sought after by these individuals. You may also find that the price may be out of your range or more than you are willing to risk. If you buy it, it is yours whether you sell it or not. In some cases, the price is just not quite good enough to make much of a profit if you tried to sell it to the interested party.

Occasionally, you can refer the item to a dealer or collector and they will reward you with a finder's fee, which can be pretty good depending on how high it may be on their want list. This could be a percentage amount or some merchandise usually agreeable to both of you. This could actually work into a partnership as you both work and look around for items for one another and thanking each other with favors or fees. I have a few arrangements where I continue and will continue to receive a "commission" on items the company sells because I introduced the original contact to them.

I had an interesting situation in which I put together an estate of an engineer/collector with a sizable home full of vintage industrial equipment, which was sold to a dealer. I received a finder's fee, which included a cash amount, along with a certain lot of product I proposed before each party spoke to one another.

Originally, I was contacted by someone about an engineer I knew. He had recently passed away. As we talked, I was able to persuade this contact to let me offer advice in the disposal of the estate. He was a close friend of the deceased, whom I knew professionally, and hired by the family to dispose of the goods left behind in the estate.

This was a large estate and not typical, as it was organized by piles. Literally every room was a pile. It was unbelievable. I was able to purchase some items right off it's always a good opportunity to buy items at a "pre-estate" sale since there is virtually no competition and you have time to think and not just grab.

This estate would have been fun to take lots of time going through and finding all of the treasures. The man was both an intelligent and interesting collector, and this was his life, work, and passion. But I did not have the time, money, or the room at that point to do so, and I could not afford to purchase the particular lot of product I received as a finder's fee at the time.

But I started to think and contacted someone through an ad I saw in a professional publication because he advertised for much of the stuff I was seeing in all of these piles, and he got excited when I described what was at the estate.

I told him I hoped there was a finder's fee involved and he assured me there was. I also told him there were certain parts in the items left in the estate I wanted, and he promised me if he was successful in the deal, they would be mine. He got on a plane and we met at the estate. He did his deal and purchased the entire contents of the house. He rented the largest rental truck you could get and hired some local boys to help him load up, which took two days. I got all I wanted—some thirty-plus boxes of equipment and several piles of books and literature—for free! He was pleased, and the estate was happy. They got cash and didn't have to work as hard removing all the stuff. I was overjoyed. If you want something, you can get creative, but then you need to watch out,

An antiques show display of interesting items.

because you just might get it.

When you know a seller, find a buyer, and put the two together, you are a broker. You are the middleman or an agent. You don't buy the product. You don't sell the product. Sometimes you get a finder's fee from the buyer or you may get a commission from the seller. If you are super fortunate, you might arrange both. You may just do it for a favor or one or more parties may give you stuff because of your help.

You can be valuable to both people. You may have built a large network of interested people in your index or directory of good contacts because of what you have learned from this book. These contacts are your edge. As you gather your index together and contact people and learn from them, you become a tremendous resource to others. You are now an expert. You cannot imagine the many ways things turn out. Learn as much as you can from all you meet. Take good notes.

When a situation arrives, say it's an entire estate or a collection or even a single important and valuable item, your first response is excitement. You see the item(s) and realize what is available. Clear your mind, inspect, and describe what is here, get model numbers, brand names, and all descriptive and condition notes possible. Try and protect the material from being sold. This is next to impossible at an open public sale—you simply have to buy it. But, if this is one of those rare and exciting pre-sale opportunities you come across, you usually have the time and space to organize and protect everything. You may want to take some photographs or a video. Be discreet with the buyer and seller, be up front and honest with each. Be careful to make all conditions and deals you wish for yourself plainly known before any introductions are made. If you see it is a good match and you are a good negotiator, you can probably make out very well without having spent a dime or handling any of the product.

As you're conversing with one person and then the next, you may be tempted to give each a little "info" on the other person. By "info" I mean subtle information like, "I know he's got the money to spend . . ." or "This guy is hoping to get an amount of $X for this stuff." This is OK as long as you are honest and don't break confidences. After all, you are the ambassador and a liaison and agent between the two. You are representing the other person in the initial stages of the deal. It's an interesting and literally rewarding experience.

What is really fun is the three-way deal: You get something, he gets something, and I get something. What a blast.

Did you really think that a small classified ad you noticed, cut out, and pasted in your index would pay off that big? Do you now understand how if you are organized and catalog your contacts this gives you an edge among all of the other pickers?

NEGOTIATE, DICKER, BARGAIN

Negotiating is fun and if you practice, you can get pretty good. Negotiating is kind of like asking for a date. You have certain lines you throw out, which can be useful. It might be about the condition of the item, or it might be a line about how little money you have right now. Or, make a comment of your experiences with that type of product. My favorite seems to be quantities or "piles" of stuff. I always grab smalls and place on the pile, and realize to me they are all actually free because they are part of the bigger deal. Sometimes you can just tell that the seller either needs a sale or just needs all of the stuff gone as quickly as possible, and can use this to help get the price lower. If you watch any of the antiques finder television shows much, you notice various negotiating techniques used over and over. We realize these shows are pretty much "scripted" for entertainment value, but you can learn some things. Watch a few shows and as you do, write down some of the lines they use and try a few out.

I recently went to an estate sale. I was late, but there was a cool antique tube "tombstone"-style radio in pretty good condition there. It was the first day and they wanted $150. Usually dealers do not give a discount until the next day or last day of the sale. I found a book I wanted for a dollar and was going to pass on the radio and just make my dollar purchase, but when I was paying for the book, the cashier said, "Just a book, couldn't find anything else?" I said, "Well yeah, but the prices are so high." She asked what in particular and I mentioned the old wooden radio downstairs, but I'd be embarrassed to make my offer, because it would be so low. She called over the "main dealer," who was probably her husband, and just blurted out, "This man would like to offer you $50 on the old wood radio downstairs." He hummed and hawed for a moment, then said okay. So I bought it. I think after my comment, she was showing that they *could* negotiate.

When negotiating, everyone's style, manners, and delivery are different, and every deal and situation will change. Much of what is said and done in a negotiation becomes subconscious and second nature. When negotiating, watch and remember what the other person says and does. He or she might be a master and your negotiations on the deal might not go as well, but you will learn much if you watch, and remember and do like he or she does next time on a different deal. Take good notes.

BEST NEGOTIATIONS LEAVE EVERYONE FEELING GOOD

If someone offers me $35 for an item I thought I would only get $15 for, I usually hesitate and think about it. I might even make a few statements about the item or pick it up and play with it. Then I finally agree. If you get excited about the offer for more money, and say, "Well yessir, I can get some more if you want," then something is suspicious. Your customer feels he went too high and just might change his mind. At the very least, he'll feel bad. The best negotiating is when both parties feel good.

If the $35 is lower than what I hoped to sell it for, I might say, "Oh no, you know, I paid more than that to get it myself." Or, even better, "If I saw one today for sale for $35, I'd buy it myself. I think I'd rather keep it for that price."

If the situation is such that you can get them to "toss something else in on the deal," here's your chance. You may have seen something of theirs that you want, just waiting for them to want something you have.

Or, how about this: "Well, that thing is something I've even considered keeping. I only really brought it along in hopes that someone really wanted it badly and made me an offer I couldn't refuse."

You can simply say, "No, you'll have to do better."

Never tell anyone you are negotiating with that you are hurting financially. They just may tempt you with some mediocre wholesale offer, knowing that you'll finally succumb to the dollars and walk away—in effect, stealing the item from you.

As you can, especially if they are buying many items from you, you might try to give them some extra items for free. These can be surplus, common, or similar things they may have shown some interest in but you consider of little value. Your customer will feel like they received a killer deal, and you get rid of dead inventory.

Negotiating is fun and actually makes you feel better. Let's look at an example:

You are trying to sell an antique player piano and give a price of $500 to someone who is interested. If this person immediately says, "Sold!" you will probably ponder afterward for a long time if you could have got a whole lot more for it.

Now, if your customer looks at it up and down, tries it out, checks around and finally says, "The best I'd probably give you is $400," you may say, "No, I need at least $450," and then at some point the deal is done at $450. He goes home smiling and thinking, "I did great. I talked him down $50." You may be thinking, "Well, that's probably all it's worth, I'm sure glad I was able to get that much for it, plus actually talk him up the extra $50." You go away counting your cool $350 profit and he goes on his way dreaming of how he'll fix it up and get $1,000 for it. You are both pleased. This was a good deal.

Don't go down in price or stick to your guns when you can see in his eyes that he really wants it and is maybe even obsessed. If you're there to squeeze every penny out of the deal, he'll go away with his buy, always wondering if you took advantage of him.

You can call it bargaining, haggling, negotiating, selling, and buying. If done with an open mind and a good attitude, you'll learn, you'll profit, and you'll gain customers and friends. You'll even enjoy it because everybody is a winner.

Isn't it interesting how much business isn't done this way? We go to the grocery store or department store and shop. If the price is too high, we may keep looking until finding it cheaper, never bothering to try and get a better deal. Can you imagine haggling over a carton of ice cream? If we just pay the price, we either are numb to the bad deal and go on, or get astonished and just complain about how hard it is to live in these times.

Some negotiators are weasels. They do it with poor form. Some just com-

HOW A CLASSIFIED AD PAID OFF

I once saw an advertisement in a magazine by a person who wanted a certain type of watch. It wasn't a rare watch, just one of those older-style electronic watches that light up with light emitting diodes or LED display. They went out of style as LCD displays became more perfected and cheaper to make.

I also knew a small service and sales company that used to sell and repair all kinds of these watches and thought that the owner might have a box of defective old watches he'd let go cheap. Although, he didn't have much in the defective stuff, he happened to have thirty brand new in original boxes, old stock LED watches. We negotiated a price of $10 a piece for the watches. As I contacted the collector who placed the ad, we decided that $25 each would work for both of us (I have no idea what he sold them for). This was a long time ago, and now they are much higher in price.

I asked him to send me a cashier's check for the amount and then I would pack up and send him the watches.

I realized $450 in quick profit from reading one ad and making one phone call. Gosh, this is better than the stock market!

plain their way through it, beg a lot, or act as if they're stupid to try and get your pity. There are also those who, because you want something, all of a sudden decide what they have is made out of gold. You could most likely find similar items just about anywhere; in fact, you do. But because you want it, it's now valuable … just walk away.

PRACTICE YOUR POKER FACE

The more hopeful, emotional, and excited you are, the more you'll pay for it. This payment can take different forms: It can be more cash; it can be that you give much more in trade to sweeten the deal; or it could be that you gave up or overlooked certain flaws in order to just have it but will be sorry about later.

Your side of the negotiation is hindered by your *wants*. Now want, in itself, is okay. You need to have wants, wishes, and goals or this stuff doesn't work.

This is a wonderful way to set up a display.
It keeps the inventory clean and easy to view.

But too much want flips into greed or obsession, which will negatively influence your decisions.

You may know that an item you are pursuing is valuable. Let's just say it is worth $1,000. You may have some items with a similar value. You know they cost you little. This might be a good trade, and an easy negotiation.

If you perceive that the other person will probably do anything to get what you have, then you usually do well in the trade. So it is obvious that if you show signs of excitement and want (or absolute lust) then you are vulnerable. That is a good reason in itself for us to not covet our neighbor's goods.

Having a good poker face is useful and if you are somewhat aloof, indecisive, or have genuine indifference, it will help you. This goes for either buying, selling, or trading negotiations.

Here's another example: An item you want to sell is marked $300, but someone offers you $100 for it. Your answer, if in an anxious state of mind, would be, "Well gosh, mister, I marked it $300." If you have a controlled answer, not caring if the guy buys it from you or not, you might say, "$100! No, that's too low. I'd rather keep the thing for $100. In fact, if I saw another one right now, I'd sure pick it up for a hundred bucks." Who's in better control?

Or, if buying something, you ask the price and are told $100 each, you answer might be, "No thank you. I usually don't pick those up unless they are cheap. I'll buy them if I see them for $40 or $50 tops." Now you are saying a couple things: You are inferring that you are some sort of a dealer and you need to buy wholesale. After all, you may, in fact, sell those retail for $100, too. You are also inferring you have in the past looked away when you saw them before at his price. He may worry that he won't possibly sell them at his asking price. You have to be willing to walk away from deals. You can't afford to pay retail if you are reselling.

When trading or bartering, you are actually shopping. Look around at the stuff as if you are shopping with cash. Place it in a pile or make a list. Tell the seller exactly what you would like. Show him what you have. Put it like

TIP: If you hang around a sale, you will hear all sorts of good approaches used by other experienced pickers and savvy buyers. There will be all kinds of good approaches and negotiation techniques and strategies used you can learn. You can also find out quickly which techniques won't work at that particular sale.

this, "For my stuff, which of the items I've selected will you let me have?" Hopefully you selected good things and several of which would satisfy the deal. He may remove a couple of items from his side. The next stage is to say, "Okay, if I toss in another three widgets, will you let me have those items?" More often than not this worked for me.

Enjoy swapping. Have fun. Try to trade up, and then go trade up again with someone else. Make a list afterward of what you gave and what you got. Put retail values to the list and see how you do. Learn from it for next time.

You will also learn a whole lot about the other person's wants. You can almost go shopping for this person when out picking. You have a new customer for certain types of product now.

When you are asked by a potential customer if you have any idea how much you want for your item, always be ready with a "yes" and then confidently state your price. Hopefully you have researched the price by then or know your stuff and can place a current value on it. You often will get what you ask.

If you hem and haw, he realizes you don't have a clue. If you are not ready to sell, tell him you need to do some more research first. I asked a dealer once after the deal was done how he came up with the price he asked and he said he priced it based only on the appeal it had to him.

MAKING THE BIG OFFER

So you found something you want to buy or you may be negotiating the purchase of an estate. Here are some things to keep in mind as you make your offer:

- Find any defects in the product and point them out to the seller.
- Communicate your experiences in buying the same items elsewhere if appropriate.
- It's always better to find their price out before you make any offer. More often than not it's lower than you would have been happy to pay.
- You may need to explain how the value to dealers (you) differs than the value to an end collector. You typically need to make at least 50 percent of the list price on something you sell. Besides, you will be expected many times to have to give your buyer a discount.
- Let the seller know how you are willing to buy the entire lot, good and bad. Explain that there is usually a whole lot of leftover stuff that is unsellable junk. Yes, it may have some value, but you won't get much for it.
- You are also taking a chance. There is a risk in time and money for you. Also explain your expenses involved.
- What if they see a catalog with high prices on stuff like they hope to sell to

you? There are those large catalog houses that do sell the items for higher prices, but realize they also offer lots of different services. They have expensive advertising to deal with. They also have the luxury of thousands of eyes seeing their ads. They have a much greater chance of finding someone, somewhere that will pay their high price.

Incidentally, at sales of all kinds you will see firsthand who the people are, and what types of things they are interested in. This is a great place to make exceptional contacts. You hear someone say, "Do you happen to have any old fountain pens?" So then you may wish to approach that person, ask for a card, and say you'll keep an eye out for fountain pens for them. Write down particulars about what they like, dislike, etc. Learn from them. Tell them what you look for and give them your card. If they have no interest in your things, they might be helpful and tell you where they think they might be found, giving you some good leads and haunts to check out. This is perfect networking. I guarantee it has great payoffs.

GOOD NEGOTIATING PHRASES TO MEMORIZE

1. "I don't usually pay that much for them when I find them." (Infers you see them around all the time for better prices, and they better lower their price if they want to sell it to you now.)

2. "I usually try and pay a lot less for my first one because if I do find another one, I will have to pay a lot more to complete the pair."

3. "Most (watches, radios, etc.,) are inexpensive, that's why I like them." (I mean, what can you say to that line? Hey, it worked on me.)

4. "What about if I throw in an extra ($20, or another widget, or...) to sweeten the deal?"

5. "I'd like to get that much for it. I guess it's because I really like the looks of it myself." (Uh-oh! They have competition breathing down their neck, and it's you! Or—They offer you a price below that which you want.) "You know what? I'd probably buy it for that price, too, if I saw another one right now, sorry," or "No, I don't think so, for that price I'd just as soon keep it for myself."

NEGOTIATING CHECKLIST

1. Always negotiate.
2. Be creative, and expect you'll make the deal.
3. Research first.
4. Remember that both of you should always win.
5. Watch out for pride and ego.
6. Don't talk too much. Know when to shut up.
7. Play it out in your mind that it works before you start. Take both sides.
8. Determine your lowest acceptable deal up front.
9. Set a goal of what you want most before you begin.
10. Watch and learn from the techniques and strategy they use.
11. Write it out on paper. How does it turn out?
12. Never give control to the other party.
13. Never assume that the price is fixed.
14. Be open-minded and listen to the other side.
15. They might give more than you hoped for.
16. Don't burn bridges. You want a good relationship in the future.
17. Never go into a negotiation assuming you won't get what you want.
18. Sometimes it just doesn't happen—walk away.

Practice these things and you will perfect your skills. Develop other strategies and add to the list. And remember, it never hurts to ask.

Be friendly with the other shoppers. So much of the time we get afraid to talk, for fear that everybody is our competition. In a way they are, but in a way, everybody is a resource, too. They may turn out to be good customers. You can gain so much more by communicating and making good friends and contacts than by what you might lose at the one sale you are at right now. Everybody has different timing or places they travel to check out. Everyone has ideas and hunches that are unique. Different pickers have varied interests,

This sign, spotted at an antiques show, takes the guesswork out of haggling for a lower price.

but their knowing what you like will benefit you in the end, as you now have more eyes and ears looking around for you. You'll be absolutely amazed what kind of a network of good contacts you'll build, whether it's for tips, good leads, or buying and selling both to and from them.

What's interesting is you will also overhear of these peoples' latest deals, where they are, and how they found out about them. You hear about people and dealers to stay away from. You are right in the thick of it and can learn a lot.

NEVER LOWBALL VALUABLE ITEMS

If you see a great piece, an important and valuable piece—one of those once-in-a-lifetime items you know you will never get a chance to buy again—you never lowball bid on it. You keep laying down the money until you can take it away. The value of an item like that now becomes what you paid for it. A big dealer in expensive quality pieces once told me that for rare items, whatever your seller wants to sell it for—you pay it.

Knowing this as a "dealer" will help you, if you ever have a chance at a major item. Realize you will get the price you want. Don't let it go for a song.

Don't fret, wondering if you will ever get your money out of it. The high-end, high-quality and expensive items always have a buyer.

Say you have an item you sell or buy by the pound. The buyer might look at the box or pile and say, "I'll give you $200 for it." Your next statement should be something like, "But there's 50 pounds there." Here's the secret: you might not even know what the stuff is or what it's worth, but saying it's 50 pounds infers you know what is there and what it's worth. It also gives a signal to the buyer that they have another chance to buy it if they raise the price, especially if they know it's worth a lot more. If it isn't worth much more, the buyer will probably tell you.

Let's put it differently. If he asks, "How many pounds are there?" and you say, "Gosh, I have no idea," he's now thinking, "He's mine! I can offer anything I want!" This works both ways, so be careful.

THE FINE ART OF CONVERSATION

Sometime you'll find out that you will do some swapping or buying or selling and realize you blew the deal because you kept talking. When the deal is done, stop. You may be negotiating and even finalize a fine trade but then you say something, and you wish your hand could fly out of your mouth after the words. I've done it.

I knew a salesman who was capable, technical, and had a great personality. He could usually handle any situation with ease and knew his stuff. The problem was he wanted to tell you all that good stuff he knew, and almost lost some good business because of it. The store where I worked received comments from customers annoyed by him and even asked us not have him come by anymore. I've done it to myself more than once, eventually giving back product when I really didn't need to, leaving dollars on the table, or

BARGAINING 'CHIP' WHEN HAGGLING

Cracks, dirt, corrosion, missing pieces, no dust jacket, no manuals, all need to be noted when negotiating. You will have the bargaining chip here. You may have another unit in the garage that "still has the knobs" or you may "have the original manual at home," etc. Don't reveal this when bargaining for the price.

any number of things. This does not mean if you hope to sweeten a deal for someone by giving a little extra that you need to stop. No, if you intend to make your customer happy on purpose, that's wonderful; it will eventually come back to you. Or, if you need to make a bad deal right and need to give back product or dollars, this is good, too. Make your customer happy by all means. Especially, when you deal with customers online, like eBay, you need to make them happy. There is an important "feedback" record kept. Always communicate with online customers quickly.

CA$H IS ALWAYS GOOD

When you pay cash for an item, it's good for a couple of reasons. First, it is a great incentive. People like cash and may be willing to do a better deal for it. They may worry about checks, especially from strangers.

Cash is also good for a level of anonymity. They won't call you back, changing their mind, etc. You don't get all the questions day after day it seems when you keep yourself anonymous. After all, they don't know whom to call.

This is a cash business. You have to keep it fluid. You need to have plenty to buy stuff. And you have to get it when you sell stuff. Watch out for credit don't take it and don't give it. When you owe money, it seems the month only lasts for a few days and the payment time is here again. Dang! When someone owes you money, it seems that weeks turn into months and months, if you ever do get paid. Today if you have a smartphone, you can easily process their credit card payment using "Square" or PayPal.

TRADING UP

If you have a quantity of some lesser value items and are able to trade for one better, higher-valued or nicer item, usually equal to or even higher to the combined value of all of your stuff, this is trading up. Trading up for you is

This sign was also spotted at an antiques show.

usually a good deal if you know the stuff you're dealing in. Trading down isn't always a good idea, unless you know you can quickly turn it for cash and it was advantageous for you to do so.

I really like to trade. It is like going to a store and having a shopping spree. You get to buy just about anything you want without spending any cash. Most of the time the other person feels he is high grading you and all the while you feel you are high grading him.

Look for items that have a high trade value or can be used as currency. Some collectibles you'll find have a steady value and can be used just like dollars when looking for products you wish to trade for.

It's usually a good idea at the end of the trade to give up one more item after you both got what want. This makes him feel good about the trade and about you. We've all heard horror stories for people who feel they have been burned by someone in a trade. They will never swap or have dealings with them again. They also tell their friends. Don't let this happen to you. A bad reputation can kill your business. A good reputation will help you succeed.

SOME ADVANTAGES OF TRADING UP

If you are a collector, the process of trading up means your collection is getting refined with better and fewer items, and you'll end up with a high value, high quality, and fine collection. If you are a dealer, this means your inventory is gathering better and higher-end stock. Your reputation improves. You might find that you don't need to spend as much time and energy selling one piece vs. many.

Remember that it may be a good idea to toss in additional lower-value items in your trade up. Your customer always feels better if you sweeten the deal. Cash can always be used as part of a trade, both on his side or yours. This is especially an incentive if what you want is really outstanding or if the items you are disposing of are slow-moving products. Her are some advantages of trading up:

1. You may have a hard time normally selling all of the lesser value items as readily as the higher value item.

2. The higher value item probably excites you more.

3. You probably have more value even if it was a straight dollar for dollar trade because you may have had to make deeper discounts on many of the lower value items to eventually get rid of them separately.

4. There is some inherent liquidity in larger ticket items, as serious collectors like the big important stuff, although it might take a while.

5. You can now have a higher plateau to trade up even higher by using this one item—much further than you could have, with the previous lot of products.

6. Remember the statement, "One man's trash is another man's treasure, er, stuff."

7. One item takes up less room than several items.

Book scout Roger Whiting scans for prices at a library sale.

Chapter 7

·····························

Picking Books a Fun Career

recently attended a large university public book sale. I really have fun at these sales. I am not a "professional book scout" by any means, but I know that in line there will be some competitive and anxious pros. They always line up early, with empty tote bins and carts, and ready with their bar code readers. Many will have several employees yanking books off the shelves, each in their assigned reading topic. They pull the book out, scan the bar code, and their handheld device will beep or chime, telling them to pull the book or leave it. They will go to the sale, knowing that the prices are $2 for hard bound, and $1 for soft bound. They program those figures into their readers and also program in a minimum value they want, for example, "not lower than $5 as found on the Amazon search for the lowest price book. When they scan the code and it's more than $5, they hear a happy chime. If it's less than the amount, they get a sad beep. They can quickly sweep all of the shelves in little time. I see these folks with dozens of tote bins filled to the brim checking out paying for their finds.

Myself, I do it a little different. I have certain topics of interest to me, or several topics I have gained some good experience selling. I look through the books on the shelf for titles, many or most will not even have a bar code. Some of these are printed before the use of ISBN numbers, which take up more time to research. I don't care, as I kind of do it by the seat of the pants. Sometimes these "vintage" titles can sell for higher prices, especially if they are more specialized or technical in nature. Meanwhile, the book scouts are passing them by, only looking for bar codes. I have been able to find some valuable gems after shelves have been swept, scanned, and stripped. My topics include some more specialized offbeat subjects that I am familiar with. Knowledge actually is power in this example.

I have also bought many worthless titles, but I feel okay about it because if I have dozens of titles I found in the same lot, which I can sell for $15-$40 each, or one book I can sell for several hundred dollars, it can offset a whole lot of $1 and $2 books. I can still sell the cheap books at a profit, anyway. Sometimes you can, for example, make a "lot" deal for a niche subject area, and sell it on eBay. You can also sell them at yard sales, swap meets, and trade them, or even donate them and receive a receipt from non-profits, which may be helpful.

I've seen lone book scouts at estate sales with their barcode scanners, but not often. Thrift stores, however, have many active scouts with scanners. Sometimes it seems they know just the right time a new cart of used books comes out into the store. (Inside deals? Nah...)

Book pickers are more commonly called "book scouts." It must be because of the specific nature of book picking and the search that the dealers have is targeted to certain titles, authors, or editions.

Book scouting seems to be in a major class by itself. Book collectors are passionate and dedicated people, and book collecting is also probably more of an "accepted" obsession. Think about it: Everyone loves good books. I even love the smell of old books. This becomes interesting in this day of electronic books. I have a couple of Kindles, and everyone in our household has an iPad and an iPhone. We all have books we can read and store on our devices or "in the cloud." But I still want a library of real books! I think there is something about having a real book on your shelf that shows ownership, and people love to and see what books you have in your personal library.

Some strange or extreme hobbies and collections sometimes raise eyebrows, even though they might be pretty interesting. You'd have to be involved to understand the reasoning and drive—but not with books. Books are a safe kind of passion. Many people in general have collectible and even some rare books in their homes.

Book collectors may start with a certain specialty and easily branch into other various topics that naturally connect to their original topic, the result of which is a constantly growing library. Serious book collectors get pretty competitive, secretive, and protective of their passion. Some are aggressive collectors as they fulfill their need to obtain books. Some feel the day is utterly wasted if they go out and don't bring back an armful or box filled with books. Many book scouts pick for themselves first and then scout for items to sell, to pay for their hobby.

Never overlook books when you are out searching for other goods. Start your own library or at least find out what books are sought after. You'll likely be in the same places the books are when you seek collectibles and antiques. You might as well get the books, too, since you can always find a buyer for good ones. You probably have a smartphone that is capable to scan and search Amazon to show you a value instantly.

Talk to others who you see scouting books all the time. Although they are your competition, you can still find out a lot by asking questions. They will tell you who the collectors or even dealers are that you can sell certain topics to locally. They will warn you of certain individuals. You might even make a good supplier or customer from these people you meet. You can learn what's hot, as they brag about certain finds they made out on. They will tell you how cheap they found something and how much they got for it. Most use Amazon to obtain their prices; others use recent auction reports to base pricing. Just by shooting the breeze with some of these folks, you can gain tons of good information.

I was watching a professional book scout one day. I have seen her pick books many times and on one particular day, I watched her as they wheeled out a new cart of books at a large thrift store. As I came up to the cart, I was probably more interested in how she worked the cart than in looking for books myself. She worked it well. She first scanned quick, grabbing and not even looking closely at what she had. At this point, condition, date of printing, first editions, signed copies, or even the price of the book was of no concern. It's just get it off the cart and away from any exposure to the competition. The high grading comes later. She quickly grabbed all she could hold in her arms. When it was safe, she reached for a shopping cart and then visually scanned each shelf at least two or three times. This was a fine-tuning effort that I noticed rendered some good titles. Then later, she looked at every book in detail before buying them. Scanning electronically would be last.

I felt I must have been a real pain to be there hovering and watching her work, but I was so fascinated in what I was seeing; I even noticed I was smiling as I watched her techniques. After the cart was inspected, she then high-graded what she found, and I'm sure she returned some to the cart. Her stack had twenty or thirty books—I had one. She knew what she wanted, knew how and where to sell them, and knew the prices. Her interests and market vary from mine, and I would not have wanted most of what I saw in her stack, but I'll bet you that if I knew more of the market, I would have wanted them, too.

A book scout's piles at a library sale.

A GOOD PICKING DAY

I had been really anxious waiting to get to a good estate sale and I recently attended one. I was able to get two full boxes of books and some miscellaneous useful and collectible inventory. I bought the entire lot for $70. The best rule of thumb is to get one item in your lot that will pay for everything. When I got home, I looked up most of the books (mainly technical and do-it-yourself titles). The first two books I was curious about what the prices were on Amazon ended up being worth what I paid for the entire lot. There was a set of technical videos that were $69.95, so I suppose that is close enough. I do not have a scanner to evaluate items on the fly. I usually use my best guess in grabbing items I am interested in, or in my own area of expertise. I think I do well. There was one fellow there that did have a scanner and was pulling off books, scanning, and piling up his load. I worked in and around where he was, and even after he left the area, I still found great items. I actually think he took too long to pull a book off the shelf, scan it, register what he saw, and place it in whatever pile he was working on. I just grabbed and piled them in my box. I high-graded a few out later. In my pile of books, I found prices listed from $.01 to $89.95, with a grand total of $500 in Amazon "value" for the books. About 25 percent of the books I did not check yet because they have no ISBN, etc. And I gave my wife five books that I did not even look up. There were also many journals, manuals, etc., which have some good value. There were also a bunch of video and film editing software packages I know nothing about. There was a new in box stereo mixer, and the pile of collectibles, and other useful items. In this pile was I believe a hand-crafted silver or nickel-silver belt buckle, a small case of fishing flies, some Olympic pins, an old box of early Boy Scouts merit badges, three old Palm PDAs, a Radio Shack Breadboard, a Cessna Sky Comp calculator, some GB Instruments electrical testers, some micro tweezers, a DVD on coin tricks, a homemade brass steam engine, and a few other cool toys. Pretty fun day out pickin'!

THE DARK SIDE OF BOOK PICKING

As you get into book scouting, it just may become obvious how serious some scouts and dealers are. You may see the same people at the same places all the time, and after awhile, it seems they know when and where the good books are going to be. Book collectors have told me that because of the fervor and competition in the book field, many times there are back-door deals that happen even in the best of places.

Libraries try and keep their sales above board as much as possible; some even try and hold preview sales for their most anxious supporters. They charge a little more at the preview sales, but it is usually worth it. The problem happens when some volunteers hide books. Sometimes they will stack them behind other books or in areas that are unlikely for people to look and then notify their culprit friends where to look when they arrive at the sale.

Thrift stores put out books at various times, and those who are pros can almost determine a schedule of when new loads come out. This is fine; those who are organized, able to schedule their time, and work hard deserve what they get. It's bad when they get a call from an insider who notifies them of the next load or where in the cart the best ones are, so they are always first. A regular guy doesn't have a chance.

Usually at an estate sale, it's anything goes. If you get to the sale first, or even the same day as everyone else, more power to you. Creativity plays a good role here. I really don't think being fair is a real concern. However, those who steal or fake prices are wrong.

Some scouts get bad reputations and are disliked by some of the stores they hang out at. One day I went to a large local thrift store. I asked about some particular books I was looking for and to my surprise, I was invited in the back room. I was able to see and choose many books before they were put out on the floor. It was mainly because they were so upset with some other regular scouts who were a real thorn in their side. Apparently, they are rude and abusive. They even knock you over as the doors are opened in the morning, knocking stuff over all the way back to the stacks. This upset them, and so they invited me to go back first. This is a gray area, maybe, but not as bad as treating the employees and other customers rudely.

Scout books for the fun and excitement. Do it for collecting and for helping your income. Consider it investing, but never do it for greed. Those who do are obvious and it is apparent why and how they operate. I really think if you have the right reasons and work hard and are nice to others, it comes back to you. Work smarter, not meaner.

As you get more and more involved in book scouting, you will begin to get a good nose for the best old books. I guess this is why I like the smell of them.

A BOOK DEALER ON BOOK SCOUTS

Let's just call him George, the local book dealer. He has a wonderful little used bookstore in a strip mall in town. He sells all subjects. He is a nice guy. He is happy, successful, and enjoys what he does.

I asked George about scouts. He says he has hired two. The rest of his books come in on trade from regular folks. These scouts know what George wants and they know what he specializes in. They know what he pays for books. He buys just about every title they bring him. They know their subjects well, and what George's customers want. They get cash or sometimes trade for what they bring in. It was also interesting to see that one of George's scouts was a literature professor at a local university. Scouts are all sorts of people.

George gets mad at collectors who come in saying, "This book lists at such and such a price in the book valuation guides, I'll sell it to you for . . ." He sends them out the door. His scouts find good stuff; make a profit, and George gets a good deal. George also makes a profit. It's a relationship. The next problem is that scouts you hire get wise, and then scout for themselves, and just sell online for their own profit. Unless it's a family business, and you are all scouting for the family, employees are difficult.

LIBRARY SALES

As I write this, I am waiting in line at a local city library sale. I am one and a half hours early. I am number six in line. Just as I got here, three more lined up behind me. This city library has a membership fee for those wanting to come early, before the public sale for their preview night. That's tonight. They have books sorted into subjects and topics. They also have their special collection area where all books in the room have more value. (They have probably checked prices on Amazon). The general sale has hard-bound books for $2 and soft bound for $1. They also have tables full of CDs and DVDs. My friend does well picking through those. There will be the regular book scouts here with their employees and totes and scanners. It's really difficult to fight against these organized and prepared scouts. My biggest beef with them is they fill a dozen totes with books, grabbing as fast as they can. Then at the end of the sale, they high grade their booty, and leave with their best finds. Regular customers won't even see those cast offs, unless they hang around. I do well with books on eBay and Amazon, but do not want to only get newer books. Besides, they don't want old pre-ISBN bar coded books. I like many of the old books, some of which bring a good return. Another seven people have lined up behind me, in the time it took to write the above words. It will be tight and competitive in there I am sure. This library and many other library sales will have prices lowered each day until the last day when they almost give them away.

I ended up buying over $100 worth of books. Many were books that I wanted for myself or my family. Some may even be given as gifts. I am probably an old school book scout and for now am delaying the temptation to get a scanner, but see I am going to probably need to get one. I noticed at this sale at least 80 percent of the people there had scanners. At least when I arrive at a sale I will scan "my area of interest" visually, then start scanning.

Some shelves at the library sale, sorted by topic.

U.S. CIVIL WAR ERA
ARTILLERY/CANNON LOCK WITH KEY
VERY RARE............$380

1950'S
MAG

If you collect in specific areas, such as vintage locks, learning all you can about them and paying attention to prices you see at antiques shows and online auctions can help you create your own price guide.

Chapter 8

....

Pricing Pointers

P rice guides are only that—a guide. They are not price books or catalogs like various industries use to set retail or even wholesale prices. You'll get an idea of a value for an item based upon all kinds of reasons. Some prices may be listed based upon prices the author saw it advertised for. Some may be what it was priced at in a store, whether or not it sold.

Prices can have big swings based on geographic areas. Your town might be in a deprived area for certain items, and the price could be high. In a different city, the same item could be way low because they're found everywhere and nobody wants them because they are hard to sell.

Prices are also as fickle as the people that buy the stuff and demand goes up and down. News on a certain item, in a magazine article, or at a major show can send buyers walking away or scrambling and frothing at the mouth, trying to locate something. You have to be involved to follow these trends. One day it's certain styles, the next it's color or brand name that drives it up or down.

Price guides are important. They have pictures, model numbers, and historical documentation. They often include finding tips and quality hints that are valuable. The description and listed information can be helpful, as well as interesting reading if it is something you are really into. Plus both the beginner and expert can use the ballpark prices listed as a guide to help them when buying, selling, and swapping stuff. It makes a good starting place for negotiations. Price, after all, is really the amount you can sell it for. Obtain all the price guides and histories on products you focus on and other areas that catch your interest to use as references. Online actual realized prices are better information, though. When searching eBay, for example, the price listed on current items is not a good guide of the value. Look instead for closed listings, shown in the left-hand column. Here again, be careful: The closed listings shown are only for a short time span. If you want information for the last year or several months, you need another tool. Subscription services like Terapeak, for example, can give you reports over longer periods of time. They can also give you many other reports on your competition, which can be valuable to know.

Some of the things I found out about Terapeak:

1. Up to 90 days of eBay selling history.
2. The best day of the week to list (end) your auction based on the item.
3. Time of day to end the auction.
4. Pricing history.
5. Highest-priced items, with photos.
6. Best duration of the auction.
7. Categories best suited for your item.
8. Historical trends.
9. Top sellers who sell the item by eBay user name.
10. International sites.
11. Product research.
12. Competition research.
13. Hot items research.

See how much money your competition sells in a given period. You can save these reports to a disk or PDF.

DO-IT-YOURSELF PRICE GUIDE

In just about any field of collectible, you will find a group of related items that have no official price guide. This can be frustrating, especially if you are new to the market. Some collectors that fervently seek these items know the models and styles and values—you are clueless. But you can start jotting down your observations in price guides and start building your own. As you read articles and ads, and as you shop, note model numbers and the prices things are selling for. The more information you gather, the better: item type, brand name, model number, and price or value are the minimum information. I use a Moleskin pocket journal for mine. I keep items I watch in alphabetical order and make a price and date notation. It's my "little black picker's book." This could also be easily done on your smartphone with an app. That will be next for me.

It does not matter that you duplicate similar models. In fact, it is preferred that you follow trends and get average selling prices. In a quick time, you will have assembled or improved a valuable and useful price catalog. More important, you'll start to see the trends in pricing and be able to keep up with the pros.

This guide, as with any price guide, is just a starting place and your mileage and price may vary.

Sometimes you find something that you think might be particularly valuable, but can't find any information about what it may be worth. One way to find out is to try and buy one. Call up someone who specializes in what the item is and ask if they have one for sale and what the price is, and if they don't, ask if they know where you can find one and what you could expect to pay for it. You'll probably find a close approximation to the fair market value of the item and you could then call around if you want to get a better average from those who know. You never have to tell them you have one on hand—you're just shopping. Playing dumb may help you here.

Now, locally, be careful. You should already have the item in your possession or have a good lock on it. You might be calling to get information from a local dealer who is working the same deal and if he gets wind of it or suspects you are after the same item, he'll quickly try to finalize the deal. In the meantime, he may also try and give you erroneous information to throw you off course.

VARIOUS FACTORS AFFECT PRICE

To figure out selling prices, you first need to realize there are many stages to understand and differentiate between them.

LIST PRICE OR RETAIL: This is the price it sells for in a store and about the limit the market will bear.

DEALER COST OR DEALER PRICE: Typically a half or third of list price. If you sell or wholesale to dealers, this is what they pay and how much you get.

COLLECTOR-TO-COLLECTOR PRICE: Yes, collectors sell among themselves. This is on par with the dealer cost and pretty close to the value something is really worth.

PICKER PRICE: Much of the time you will find stuff at ten cents on the dollar or better. This is how much you buy stuff for when you are out foraging at the sales.

FREE: It happens!

A couple of diverse but clean groupings of items.

You will be involved with all of these prices. You profit by wholesaling to dealers, selling to collectors, and even sell or trade at retail values. Try not to get too hung up on where the deal is on the scale—as long as you turn your inventory and make a profit.

Everyone hopes to buy low and sell high. Some deals are unbelievably profitable, but some you lose on, too. The main goal should be to just keep finding better sources, contacts, and customers. Always be looking for better stuff. You can always make more money by turning your inventory than by trying to get your highest dollar out of every find.

When you have an item to sell, there is a lot to think about when there are many different factors that can affect the price. There are also many factors you might feel could affect the price, but have no real bearing on the value of the object.

1. ARE YOU EMOTIONALLY ATTACHED IN ANY WAY TO THE ITEM?

If you are attached emotionally, watch out. You will probably ask for too much and not be able to sell it. If it belonged to a deceased parent, your best friend gave it to you, or it was a Christmas present from your first-born child, to someone else that means nothing—no one else has the bonded value you feel.

2. IS IT HISTORICALLY SIGNIFICANT, AND DO YOU HAVE PROOF OR DOCUMENTATION?

Now here's where those bonding values do reach out to others. The item may have a story. It may have been used in a movie or a celebrity previously owned it. Maybe it is a prototype unit handmade by the inventor. But you still have to watch out, as it could be a fake. You might not be able to prove the previous ownership and hearsay doesn't last. You need documentation, autographs, letters, photos, and other proof. With such documentation, the value can be much higher.

3. HAS IT BEEN REPAIRED OR RESTORED? IS IT WORN AND USED, OR IN MINT CONDITION?

You need to inspect the items you buy and sell for cracks, errors, repairs, and fakery. Be careful when you buy and be up front and disclose all you know when you sell. It is horrible to sell an item and later find out the buyer wants to return it because you weren't clear on a description. The best thing is to sell as is, as found, untested. Don't try and pass off obvious errors.

4. IS THE ITEM COMMON?

Commonly found products won't bring the value rare items will. Some good products and nice antiques are common and have low values. Sometimes these low values are regional. Sometimes they are hard to find in other areas of the country or even different countries and demand higher prices.

5. IS THE ITEM OLD, CLASSIC, OR BECOMING VINTAGE? COULD IT BE A PRE-COLLECTIBLE?

Certain items do have a lot of potential for future collectible products. Savvy investors can do well if they choose these items and tuck some away in hopes for collectible values. Be careful.

6. IS IT THE RIGHT COLOR, AESTHETIC, OR PLEASING TO LOOK AT? IS IT FUNKY OR WILD?

Old antiques are interesting, beautiful, and have classic lines. They are pleasing to the eye. Craftsmen made them and their art is lost. Art Deco items, for example, have a look that is interesting and sought after; the '50s have a kind of crazy look and feel that baby boomers remember. These styles have to be learned and recognized. Once you understand different types and lines, you can pick them out and have a better feel for the values and prices as you buy and sell.

7. DO YOU LIKE IT? WHAT WOULD YOU PAY FOR IT? (WHAT DID YOU PAY?)

As a consumer, you can tell a lot about prices. Sometimes you just have to price it based on a gut feeling or by the value it has to you.

8. DO YOU HAVE ABUNDANCE IN YOUR INVENTORY? IS IT SOMETHING EASY OR DIFFICULT FOR YOU TO SELL? WOULD YOU LIKE TO DISPOSE OF THE MATERIAL? DO YOU NEED THE CASH?

These are reasons to take less profit and price lower.

9. DO YOU HAVE A READY CLIENTELE THAT WILL BUY THIS PRODUCT ANYTIME YOU FIND IT?

If so, you can usually set your price, but be careful you don't upset the deal by taking advantage of them. You stand to lose if you are greedy. Serious collectors realize you have to put your dollars down and buy it.

10. HAS THERE BEEN A FAVORABLE WRITE UP IN A NATIONAL MAGAZINE OR BOOK ON YOUR ITEM? HAS IT BEEN THE FEATURE PRODUCT IN A MAJOR COLLECTOR'S SHOW?

When an item is famous, interest is piqued and demand is high, and this is usually an opportunity to take advantage of a bit more profit for it.

11. DO YOU KNOW MUCH ABOUT THE PRODUCT?

If you don't, about all you can do is copy prices you have seen elsewhere and hope they are right. Or take the time to study the market and learn more about what you have. If it is a rare and important piece, maybe an appraisal is in order.

12. WHAT ARE OTHERS SELLING THEM FOR IN YOUR AREA?

Regional values will vary greatly. East Coast, West Coast, all areas have a different supply and demand. Some areas might have a larger supply of an item because it was produced there. However, demand might be higher because the historical significance is greater there, too. Many collectors in that area may have worked at the manufacturer, or had parents work there, etc. They may specialize in that particular brand, etc. Compare with the national market price if possible.

13. IS THERE A WAY TO GET SOME SORT OF AN OFFICIAL APPRAISAL ON THE ITEM?

Sometimes you can get an appraisal by asking the right questions. For example, you can take the approach that you are looking to buy an item and ask, "How much would I have to pay for one of these if I found one?" If you ask this of enough dealers, you might get a good idea of the value of the item.

An official appraisal by a qualified and honest person will usually cost you something. Always get it in writing on their letterhead and attach all of your documentation, photos, etc.

14. HAVE YOU NOTICED SOME APPRECIATION OR DEPRECIATION IN THE PRODUCT IN THE CURRENT MARKET?

If prices are sliding, it might be well to investigate and maybe dump what you can now. If the prices are climbing, hold onto what you have as an investment.

HERE ARE SOME THINGS THAT CAN AFFECT AN ITEM'S WORTH:

- Condition
- Authenticity
- Documentation
- Proof
- Previous owner
- Needs of seller
- Want of buyer
- Hype
- Market value
- Advertised value
- Prestige and status
- Rarity
- Historical importance
- Investment
- Value
- Supply and demand
- Competition
- Value added
- Quality
- Beauty
- Aesthetics
- Model type
- Prototype
- Ability to pay

Antique glass Aladdin lamps.

Here are some other steps helpful in evaluating something you have found:

First of all, you need to identify the item. Look for brand names, model numbers, etc., and also note that certain colors and styles do make quite a bit of difference in values. See if there is a price guide available on the products. You may even need to research it in the original manufacturer's literature. Try and find an expert.

Many times just calling a dealer or two can help you find the most knowledgeable collector in the field. Some magazines have extensive classifieds, which have for sale and wanted advertisements that can help you make valuations. Auction reports can also list same or similar products and the prices they were sold for. Some dealers send out catalogs and lists containing prices of items they wish to sell. These can be helpful to compare for current market prices. Remember that condition has the biggest effect on pricing.

On the other hand, sometimes you just have to take your best offer, even if it isn't as good as you originally hoped for. If you have had something for a long time and have no other offers, the bird in the hand may be your best bet.

Don't get hung up on the price. There are many prices. There's your cost. There's the wholesale price. The current market also has a certain value or price. There is the asking price and the actual selling price.

KNOW THE MARKET

Antiquities and collectibles are a risky but potentially interesting and lucrative business. Let's look at a scale of time as it might relate to antiques and collectibles:

1. Antiquities (prehistoric artifacts).
2. Antiques—over 100 years old.
3. Antiques—less than 100 years old.
4. Collectibles—fairly recent, memorabilia, nostalgia, vintage.
5. Pre-collectible—recent items, no real trend yet, but interesting from a hobby or décor standpoint.

If you can predict or foresee an item or group of products as classics, potentially collectible, or sleepers, you might just be able to cash in on a pre-collectible. You may be able to corner the market on items now while people are throwing them away—before they get hot.

The key is to find items that have just gone out of style or are being replaced by newer, better products because the usefulness is gone. It might be readily available now at low prices and in quantity. Nobody is buying and there is no interest. Look for innovative items such as the first new type of toy. But watch out—it might never take off. You might have all your money tied up in a warehouse of garbage.

Realize that if stuff is now showing up at sales and swaps cheap, it also means a much larger quantity is being tossed into the garbage. This disposal might be to some a disaster, but in reality gives increasing value to the items left.

Some fairly recent examples that may have surprised some people include:
• Miniature reel-to-reel tape recorders
• L.E.D. watches
• Electronic L.E.D. pocket calculators

These were somewhat recently considered junk, but now can be valuable.

Realize that some seem to have a vision of what will be a collectible. They may have some forceful influence in how the market grows. It well could be that they drive the interest to where it is. First they collect, then hoard, document, write newsletters, start clubs, establish prices, and even print books on the subject. Many interesting stories are written, wanted classified ads start showing up, museums are formed, and feverish trading builds the craze.

Unbelievable prices start being quoted. Before you know it, these items are a full-blown collectible. Soon others with some foresight gain interest and gather products and become dealers and experts. An entire economy is built— even livelihoods are maintained from what was junk and is now treasure.

When you are first introduced to some pre-collectibles, you may feel some disbelief at what is popular and maybe your parents or grandparents even had lots of the items that you used to just play with or take apart. You start searching the basement or garage of your folks' house and may discover some items. You might even find the best of the best as far as what everybody is wanting in the new field. Then you find others, make contacts, and start picking for them and trading, and maybe collect a few for yourself. Sometimes you get hooked. There is a fine line between picker-dealer and collector. Nostalgia is a big element at play here. People get emotionally attached to items and memories. Some of this stuff really gets important to them.

We find things that we had no idea existed—things that were common at the time but now forgotten and disposed of. To piece together history is a rewarding and exciting adventure for some.

As more and more get involved in collecting, some things gain higher popularity. Models become more valuable because they have a certain classic look. Features are pointed out in magazine articles. Rarity is discovered. The harder it is to find certain items, the more people want them and values soar.

As I write this, some of the mentioned pre-collectibles are well on their way to becoming full-fledged collectibles. Some have prices bordering antiques. Look at pocket calculators or even slide rules. They both apparently started their rise to collecting within the scientific community. Values are rising and

IDENTIFYING THE NEXT POSSIBLE PRE-COLLECTIBLES

So, what will be the next craze, the next pre-collectible? How are you going to find it or how can you be involved and become an expert in the field once it is identified?

1. Be interested in it yourself. It has to hit a nerve.
2. Read magazines and books on collectibles.
3. Talk to people in clubs, other pickers, dealers etc., and ask what else they collect and what's hot.
4. Go to shows and learn.
5. Send for mail-order catalogs and lists from classified ads.
6. Read the wanted columns, take notes, and review them.
7. You might have knowledge and interest in an area that could initiate and drive a new market.
8. You may have a friend or relative who is crazy enough to have a large collection of just the stuff you are looking for.
9. Something neat you have already been buying every time you see it. I guarantee someone somewhere else is, too.
10. Continually research eBay, Amazon, collector's forums, and blogs online.

good models are becoming scarce compared with a short time ago.

The people who used these products daily in their work are familiar with the brands and features and remember shopping for them. They also remember how much they wished they could have had certain ones but couldn't afford them at the time. Now they find them at swap meets for pennies on the dollar. They have by now finished college and have careers. They also know the things that have replaced these old dinosaurs, but they still have a tender memory of the items and buy them because they still like them. They also recognize that today's manufacturing processes aren't as interesting as the old way. It's fun to look back at how they used to make stuff—bigger, heavy, ugly, beautiful, funny, and absolutely classic. They don't make stuff like that anymore. You can go back in time when you assemble a small collection and see the innovation change model to model. The quality and craftsmanship and weight is different. The way it looked is different. It's historic, archaic, and wonderfully nostalgic.

Notice how competition drove innovation to more complex, sleeker, and more massed-produced items that are not as interesting and good as the old stuff.

I had a conversation once with an old-timer, who said he had a shop that repaired large quantities of radios in the 1930s and 1940s. His company would take in radios, fix them up, and call later to find out the customer had replaced it with a better or more modern and stylish radio and were not interested in returning to pick up the old one. This might have been a cathedral radio or a Bakelite or a floor console, but it was junk as far as this customer was concerned. It was also junk as far as this repairman was now concerned. He lost the profit of the repair bill. He couldn't possibly sell the old-fashioned used ones, and did not know that forty or fifty years later these things would be so precious. Since it was impossible to warehouse them, many trips were made to the landfill with large loads of wooden and plastic radios—radios that are now considered classic. The repair bills were probably $10 to $12 a piece. Now these jewels are worth $100 to $500 or even thousands.

So we see now why they are collectible. The cycle that made them worthless and subsequently tossed away actually caused them to increase in value because they are now harder to find.

The growth of new collectors also helps the value climb, as more items are increasingly wanted, but less is found. It's tragic on the one hand that an antique or collectible is now a prize because a hundred or a thousand just like it have been disposed of, buried deeply in the trash heap.

HELP ME SELL ON EBAY

Occasionally I get a phone call or contact from a neighbor or a friend of a friend who has heard that I make my living selling stuff on eBay. They hate their job, can't find work, or have some ideas that this would be the life. My first response is: "What is it you want to sell on eBay?" They are usually silent or respond with, "What do you think I should sell?"

I then go through the following:

1. Have you ever bought anything using eBay?
2. What do you have right now that you would like to sell?
3. Do you have any hobbies?
4. What are you collecting right now?

A rare antique Mickey Mouse radio with original box spotted at Brimfield.

5. What kinds of things are you excited about and really have an interest in?

6. What do you do for a living? What do you really know a lot about?

7. Do you know how you will be handling shipping and mailing?

I explain how you really need a passion in something. An example could be that you are a chef in a restaurant, and know about cooking and the tools used to cook. So, go find a bunch of kitchenware, either new wholesale surplus, or antique rare kitchen items. You could be a retired Air Force pilot, and antique militaria collectibles, or even surplus aircraft parts could be your thing.

Here are more examples:

- **DENTIST:** old dental or dental lab equipment
- **CONSTRUCTION WORKER:** antique tools, close out new tools
- **FEDEX DRIVER:** transportation memorabilia and advertising collectibles
- **ELECTRONIC ENGINEER:** old radios and electron tubes and test equipment
- **CHEMIST:** labware and supplies, even chemicals
- **GEOLOGIST:** rocks minerals fossils
- **ARTIST:** art, supplies, etc.
- **DISTRIBUTOR** (For anything! Ask your boss if you can sell the old, slow-moving inventory for a percentage).

If you have interest in something, someone else does, too, and there are categories for just about anything. If someone has a hard time deciding what his or her interests are, just go through the list sometime, it's amazing.

If you could own your own museum, what would you fill it with?

What did you like as a child?

What did your father do for work?

What influences and encouragement did you receive from your mother?

Do you have any unique sources that only your geographic area has?

There are large antiques shows, swap meets, and trade shows in many areas of the country and you could have a never-ending supply of great products to sell.

Are there any large or unique surplus outlets in your area? Many large universities have their own surplus store, and some government agencies have "property redistribution" outlets.

Do you know where all the antiques malls are?

Do you follow Craigslist? Is there any other local online classifieds that are active areas for people selling stuff? Do you know of any local Facebook swap or classified selling tools? Many of these online resources are valuable, not only to find items, but also to quickly resell or "flip" the stuff you have to sell. Local classifieds are great to sell larger items you do not want to package and ship. You can also offer trades for items you are interested in. Some of these resources have the ability to send you a notice through an RSS feed or even through smart phone app notifications. This way you can find stuff faster than the occasional browser. The online classifieds are important for you to advertise for items you want to buy. People will bring you stuff!

There are always auctions somewhere. Find out where all the auctioneers are in your area. Get signed up for notifications of upcoming auctions. Get signed up on everything you can, and this goes for estate sale dealers, too. I am on so many lists right now, I have a little trouble deciding where I want to go next.

At some point, you will discover you will need space. You might be fortunate to have a large home, with a big empty garage or out building or basement. Some people build sheds; some have barns, and some people work out of storage units. I did for a while, but it was too expensive to continue. I am fortunate that I have access to a warehouse, but even a warehouse can have challenges with shelving, losing stuff, etc.

As far as shipping and mailing, make use of the US Postal Service flat rate boxes. They are an excellent value. I have shipped some heavy items for a small percentage of what it would cost to ship by FedEx or UPS. I also ship large, but lightweight, packages via USPS Parcel Select. UPS will charge extra for larger dimensions and you need to study and understand how this works. It's pretty frustrating to sell a big, lightweight item on eBay and find out UPS is now charging you for 30 pounds instead of ten pounds like was in the eBay listing. It can eat up your profit fast. I usually always use media mail for books, CDs, and DVDs. But check, because First Class mail can save money on lighter things. I usually get all of my boxes free, and much of my packaging, too. Check what is available locally by searching for packaging companies. For US Postal Service mailings, I use Endicia for my desktop postage service. Stamps.com and others have similar products.

KNOWLEDGE IS POWER

I had a conversation with my wife's aunt one day about searching for antiques and collectibles to collect and sell online and I suppose I was too exuberant and a little boastful about some of my better deals. I had had a successful run on eBay for a few months and was pretty surprised at what I had been able to sell, and how much money it was bringing in. As we talked, she said, "Oh, I wish I could follow you around someday and see how you do it!"

This got me thinking that it would probably be impossible for her or anyone else to figure out what I was doing just by following me around and watching me. I see stuff that I immediately know about, because:

Marbles and card games for sale at an antiques show.

1. I have or have had one, sold one before, or needed one.
2. I have seen it online or in one of the many magazines or catalogs I receive for research.
3. Personal collections I've seen.
4. Museums I have visited.
5. Trade shows I have attended.
6. My work or professional background and experience.
7. My hobbies, interests, and tastes.
8. Books I have read.
9. My superior intelligence…
10. All the deals I've made over the years, people I know, etc.

Let this be a lesson for new or learning pickers: Knowledge is power. Read, research, and be interested in various topics; becoming an expert.

If you worry and wonder if other pickers are going to follow you around getting your secrets and find all the stuff you hope to get, think again. Think of all the times you go somewhere and *don't* see that guy. You have different venues, a different timetable, etc. Even if they were right behind you, chances are pretty good they would not have a clue of the things that you find interesting or valuable. I believe this world if full and there is enough stuff for everyone. Then, in this business, things get sold again after the previous owner dies. You won't have enough money to buy everything good you see. Your truck is not big enough. Your basement, garage, storage unit, and warehouse are never going to be big enough.

HOW I LOST THOUSANDS OF DOLLARS

I started selling and buying on eBay several years ago. I delayed doing this for so long out of laziness I suppose. One major experience showed me what I was missing and taught me a major lesson.

I once drove out of state with some friends to an estate of an avid camera collector and ended up with a nice vintage collection. There were early Leicas, early medium format cameras, and lots of classic gear. I did keep what I thought was the best part of the collection, and took dozens of collectible cameras to a camera "picker number one." He selected about a dozen cameras, high-grading me, and I made my money back on the collection. I felt pretty smart since I got to keep the good stuff for free, sold a bunch, got my money back, and had more cameras to sell. So then I went to another camera "picker number two." This guy hates picker number one and was disgusted when he heard that picker got some cameras before he did. But he bought the rest from me and I made a bunch more money. Boy, was I smart! On the way out of his home, I noticed on his desk a computer printout from eBay. It was easy to remember his seller name, so I became curious. About a week later, I notice all of these cameras I had sold him were listed! Cool! I'll see how much they sell for. To my surprise, and later anguish, the auctions ended and I saw he made over $700 profit on the cameras I sold to him. He got third dibs, after I kept the first group and sold the second group, and he still profited $700! What on earth did I sell to camera picker number one? I immediately signed up for eBay and started selling, and one of my first sales was for a set of salt and pepper shakers made in Japan. I got $175 for them and thought, You have got to be kidding me!

BEST TIME TO END AN AUCTION FOR ANTIQUES PICKERS

When do you think is the best time to end an auction on eBay? Some people I have asked feel certain days are better. Here is what I have found in my own "straw poll" for between 6-10 p.m. PST:

Sunday **30%**
Monday **22%**
Tuesday **18%**
Wednesday **7%**
Thursday **18%**
Friday **0%**
Saturday **5%**

When I look for items to sell on eBay, I often search for items "in quantity." These are great for putting in your "buy it now" eBay store. They are best left "good until cancelled" and left working 24/7 getting a sale occasionally, which helps pay the bills. The auction is best for rare one-of-a-kind antiques. The auction is also great for getting rid of stuff, either in singles or in lots. I use the auction for single items that I have no idea in the world what they are. Start the auction low to gain more exposure and views.

Flea markets have tools you can use yourself, as well as other items for resale.

Vintage cameras are popular with international buyers, so enterprising pickers can find a market for any they come across.

Chapter 9

·····························

Surplus Inventory and Other Opportunities

H ere's an interesting slant on picking, but it really works for some. Many stores, distributors, and some manufacturers all accumulate extra, unsold inventory. Inventory just sitting hurts the bottom line and ties up cash. Many times markets change and their customer's desires result in this unwanted merchandise. These companies get stuck with all sorts of excess product. It might be finished goods or the parts and pieces that they make the product with. Understand that these companies have written off or marked down these items to zero cost. You can usually offer any price and they will take it.

As a picker, you can approach this in several ways. If you have the cash and the customer base, you might want to contact a certain company and ask for a list of its dead or slow-moving inventory. Many times it is a quick computer report that will list what was paid for it originally. You can then contact other similar companies that might have current use for it and make a healthy profit.

Another way to work it is to contact one of the many organized liquidation companies informing them of your expertise in your field and ask about working on commission, if you find certain products or buyers for their products. Some people even set up small companies with the word liquidator in their name and send out cards and letters in quantity to stores and distributors telling them what they are looking for, and asking for samples. Then they contact the real liquidator with their find and put together a deal using other people's money and making a good profit.

TIP: FOLLOWING UP ON OLD LEADS

Do you ever "just have a feeling" you should call one of your old leads, who "has a bunch of ... " or a collector or dealer, or anyone who may be a good contact for items you deal in or collect?

I was recently in a different city on business and remembered a note in my "hot leads" file of a collector in a city half way between where I was working, and my home. I called and a woman who answered asked who I was, and how I knew the man of the house. She shocked me when she said he had died the previous week and they were cleaning out the house right then, so I had better come over. I went by, still in shock, and ended up filling my car to the top with items I collect and sell. There was no competition, the prices were low, and I was a big help to her.

Or you could simply be a liquidator, if you have the cash, time, and warehouse space to store and process the items you'll start finding.

As I am out picking, I see many other people picking some weird stuff. I also see them pass by stuff I am looking for, which amazes me. I've seen them carry around boxes and baskets of stuff I would not think twice about, and they are ecstatic and walk around as happy as larks. I'm sure people have seen me in the same way as they see my load of trash thinking I'm a crazy man, but if I can sell my find and double or triple my money, I never feel crazy. If they're doing the same ... wow!

SCRAP METALS CAN BE GOOD MONEY

I know several people who deal in various stages of electronics collectibles who also make an absolute fortune in scrap metals and precious metals. Sure, they sell the old radio tubes and parts, but they have discovered there is gold, silver, platinum, palladium, copper, aluminum, and other scrap that is worth cash. Old computer boards and relays and parts have various amounts of valuable gold and silver contacts and plating.

Various refiners will buy it in bulk and process it for a percentage if you assemble a large amount to ship to them. Often government auctions have bags and boxes and pallets of items containing such products.

If you had about 200 pounds (about three small buckets of good clean pins), it would yield about seven ounces of gold. Look at today's gold prices to figure the value. Electronic relays have tiny contacts in them that have platinum, gold over silver, solid gold, and palladium metals.

If you were finding similar types of products, it would be well to research this area to find more profit in stuff you might have available. I wrote a detailed ebook, *E-Waste Gold*, that details more about this fascinating way to do some industrial picking, and is available at Amazon.com.

GOLD TREASURES

A friend of mine told me a great story of how he was at an estate sale and found an old box with some dental picks, tools, and other items. He thought they looked old and useful, so he bought the box for $15 or $20. Guess what? As he was looking through the box (or, dare I say, "a picker picking through the dental picks"), he found several gold teeth that were later refined and sold for hundreds of dollars.

This same thing happened to me about two months later. I heard from another friend that someone he knew had items I go after that he was wanting to get rid of. I made an appointment, saw the stuff, filled up my entire trunk for $25 and drove home. When I started going through the boxes, throwing away stuff, finding regular stuff, and an occasional neat thing or two, there it was: a gold dental bridge of about four teeth just shining up at me. In this box of old dirty hardware was about a half an ounce of gold!

If this much was found here in our little area, can you imagine all the garages and basements in larger areas that have old junk in them that have little forgotten treasures like this? I'll bet that in any large city there is hundreds of old coffee cans with some gold teeth or coins just sitting in them. Are you excited yet?

REPLACEMENTS, LTD.

Did you know that there are companies that supply people with replacements for all of the priceless and irreplaceable dishes and glasses and silverware that is lost or broken? One large such supplier is Replacements, Ltd. in Greensboro, NC. The company has an immense warehouse filled with product and nearly 50,000 items per day are processed. These can be recent, antique, or rare patterns. The company's annual volume approaches $60,000,000 per year.

Where does it get many of the pieces to complete Grandma's set of china or silverware? From an organized network of thousands of pickers located all over the country. The way they hire these pickers is to sell them a subscription to a catalog and price guide they publish. This catalog lists thousands of patterns they are seeking and the prices they will pay if you find them.

This is just one of many such businesses (albeit, one of the largest) that provide a service like this and require an army of pickers to gather their inventory.

MAKE YOUR STUFF A STAR

I know of a few collector/dealers who rent the antiques and collectibles in their collection for movie props. I read an article about a collector who has a collection of over 50,000 modern artifacts and rents items to photographers for props and makes about $50,000 a year doing so.

They simply make available to certain movie production companies in their area information on the stuff they specialize in and have in their collection. They usually have enough contacts and friends who collect that they become a valuable resource to the film industry. These things, of course, are all done under the protection of a good contract. The renter is responsible for damage and loss. They also offer historical research and consulting, so the film people get it right.

These folks have big budgets for this stuff and you can make quite a good fee for the rental of especially rare items. If they do buy the stuff from you, they usually pay exorbitant prices.

TIP: AVOID BRIGHT COLORS

Bright colors at yard sales are a dead give away. When you are to that point in the day, you've already done well at an estate sale or two, and now you are "yard sailing" it back home, you don't need to stop at every one you see. My opinion only, but I have determined that for good finds on vintage stuff, you can drive right on past any colorful yard sales. It's usually kids clothing, kids toys, and newer worthless products. Look for darker subdued, older displays.

LISTEN TO THAT LITTLE VOICE

Recently I wanted to check out a shop for rock hounds. At least 20 years ago, I was active in collecting rare minerals. I knew about this particular store locally for many years, but just never took the time to go inside. I had a brief thought go through my mind that when in the area, I should go look inside. I looked around, saw some things that brought back many fun memories, and looked at prices, etc. Price knowledge is good information, in case I ever want to sell my collection. There was another man in there looking for someone to help him sell an entire shop of lapidary tools and boxes of rocks, and more. The picker in me jumped to attention and I offered to give him some guidance. As of this writing, we still need to get together and see what he has. What are the chances of that happening? Follow that little voice inside of you. You never can guess how, when, or in what way you will be led to opportunities.

LOOK FOR HIDDEN SOURCES

When dealing with bulk collectibles, these types of deals are usually limited to friends or contacts calling out of the blue, "Hey, would you be interested in a bunch of ... ?" If you have the time and are creative, you can search for some of these opportunities. Don't limit yourself to garage sales, swap meets, or even estate sales. Branch out looking for new and normally hidden sources. You might be interested in buying and selling industrial surplus. Call around and ask questions. Some places you might call are:
• Manufacturing firms, or assembly houses
• Distributors
• Scrap dealers
• College and universities surplus centers
• Government surplus depots and stores
• Local scrap refiners

If you contact these people, ask lots of questions and see where it leads you. You might find dead ends, but you will learn a great deal of information and pick up new terms you can use in the next conversation. You will soon seem like you know what you are talking about and get new names and contacts. By not giving up, you'll soon find the right person who could literally lead you to a gold mine—both in information and in products. Please note, this works whether you are buying or selling items. It also works for many industries and fields of interest, so get your yellow pages out, think of every likely resource you may have, and start calling. You never know where it might lead you.

TIP: ANTIQUES AND COLLECTIBLES PRICE GUIDES

Build your own price spotter's guide. Get a small pocket address book with index tabs. Keep eBay favorite searches going on items you specialize in. Write completed prices realized on the eBay sale in your index i.e. brand, model number, etc.; $47, $32, $150, etc. This is your price guide you can take with you when hunting for these items. Amazon-found prices are also added to your spotter's guide for your favorite items.

IT'S SMART TO SPECIALIZE

Is there a hobby or interest you had when young that you would like to resume? Are you trained in a certain area that could lend an expertise to something collectible, i.e., you are a computer technician and might go after the early computer or calculator market? Do you have special memories for certain old things of your past? Do you have a large resource available that is unique to your culture or locality or historic area, sich as Amish, pioneer, railroad, treasure, nearby historical manufacturer, etc.?

Being a specialist in a particular field is the best and first way to enter the market. It is best to know all you can about one particular type of item, whether glassware, toys, military memorabilia, or some really unique and off-the-wall subject. Buy all of the books you can find and read about the subject. Subscribe to magazines dealing with the items. Join clubs, visit museums, read blogs, and find other collectors and dealers. Ask questions and learn. Get familiar with prices, condition, etc. Recognize quality, model numbers, varieties, dates, and all you can about the best items. Know the rare and expensive pieces. Look for fakes, reissues, and reproductions.

After this, you can become familiar with the spin-off or closely related fields of your specialty. The reason is, many of the collectors who go after the first level also collect and trade between other levels and related products. An example could be that your specialty is Victrolas and antique phonographs. A related or second level might be records or radios. Several collectors collect all of these. The next level may be televisions or telegraph items. Do you see how these are all related? Collectors then collect books for these fields.

Next, you should familiarize yourself with other general collectibles and antiques and with cash-producing finds. It is great when you're out looking for your particular items and find a salable cash-producing treasure. The beauty of it is that because it's not your thing, it isn't hard to let go. You can easily sell it and get money to invest in your specialty.

It is handy to know a little about lots of various industries. Commonly, book scouts work this way. After all, right next to the book that you want is likely a book you can sell quickly. So target and immerse yourself in your narrow field of interest, then branch out. Open yourself up to other possibilities to make a profit by searching the ads and looking for what all sorts of things people find interest in. You will find dealers and collectors who are anxious to get stuff you might have been passing up every day.

VINTAGE IS BIG OVERSEAS

An interesting phenomenon is how people in especially Asian countries are eagerly buying large amounts of vintage products from the U.S., including clothing, audio equipment, and collectibles of many types.

I wondered what the big secret was, and talked to certain dealers and a few traveling Japanese buyers who come here to find products. The simple explanation is that it is a fad—almost a cult wish to have this stuff. Some pickers are making an extreme fortune in selling to these folks.

After World War II, Japan was a relatively poor country and a typical wage per day was around $1 for laborers. Lots of items made in Japan were shipped abroad to the U.S. and other wealthier countries. These people could not afford the items they saw and heard about, so today, there is a strong nostalgia for many of these vintage items that they could not have in these earlier poorer times. The Japanese people have a different economy now. They have disposable income and they spend it. Those collectors who love this old American stuff have driven the prices up here and abroad—and most of it is just because they want to show off to their friends.

I met a Japanese buyer who travels here several times a year. He has a truck and a US warehouse. He knows the likely places to visit and is essentially an international picker. This man is organized and has a large clientele, and he has loads of cash with him. He's here for at least a month each trip, gathering and shipping stuff to a friend's warehouse. He then boxes it all up in a container and ships it home where his large warehouse and customers stand waiting.

In Japan, there is even a magazine devoted to Americana for fervent collectors. Another interesting side note is that there are many Japanese-made items that were exported to the U.S. that Japanese collectors are desperately seeking.

Where does it all end?

Picking Terms to Know

This is not just a regular old glossary. These are great idea peg words. Review these terms occasionally and you'll find you get lots of good ideas and plans.

ANTIQUED: Not really antique, but new products that are made crudely or rustic in mass production to look like they are old and important. These are usually decor items. Some antiques stores have their entire store filled with this stuff.

BIRD-DOGGING: A good "bird-dogger" can find a prize in the rough. You ask questions, get leads, dig a little bit further, try more ideas, and look in more places. This separates the great pickers from all of the regular folks. There is an old saying that says: "Even a blind hog finds an acorn once in awhile, but you've got to be rooting around." You seem to have a nose for it. A good bird-dogger can also be called a good "noser."

CLASSIC: You can tell a classic when you see it. Classic items to those who have developed an eye for them seem to speak. It has to do with a combination of nostalgia, esthetics, a good knowledge of art and history, and refined tastes. You might have that appreciation grow by seeing an item that you had or saw as a child. Many times you can tell by heft, or weight combined with quality, details, and craftsmanship. This along with period or age brings out the classic items.

CLOSET COLLECTOR: A low-profile collector who collects for their own enjoyment, with not a lot of others knowing they collect much of anything. They are not too involved in clubs, shows, or other public displays with their collection. It might be a security concern they have or it could be they just prefer privacy. Once in awhile the only time the collection is seen is when the person's estate is for sale.

COLLECTIBLE: Just about anything is, has been, or will be collectible, including items that are manufactured or found naturally. Certain people like to collect items within a specialty or several specialties.

DUMPSTER DIVING: Not really picking per se, but many items that end up for sale at swap meets and even some dealers shops may have been discovered in a dumpster somewhere.

EARLY BIRDS: Folks who get the worms. You'll see ads for estate and yard sales that demand no early birds. Usually they mean the sale begins at 9 a.m. and they don't want people coming by at 7 a.m. before the crowd pounding on the door wanting to sneak in before everyone else. You should always plan your day to be out early in order to find the best stuff. It's always better to be polite at the sales.

EPHEMERA: Paper collectibles including paperwork, brochures, catalogs, and literature. These are many times important history and documents that can be especially valuable. Much of the original paper was to be temporary, and disposed of.

ESOTERIC: The explanation given to people that means you are not in the loop or just would not understand pertaining to some collectors' interests.

FAUX: Phony or fake. Some suppliers try to be sneaky and use this fancy word to hide the fact that their product is a rip-off or a reproduction.

FEEDING FRENZY: When pickers and others pile into a small area and push, shove, and grab all the goodies before the other person can. Blood is pumping, eyes are looking back and forth, and grubby little fingers are frantically pawing through the goodies. It can be either exciting or exasperating.

FLEA MERCHANT: Someone whose livelihood is to buy items to sell at flea markets. A flea merchant also finds gray market products, usually including factory seconds and overstock merchandise to sell. You might be surprised to see how many manufacturers and distributors in your areas sell to flea merchants to dispose of their unwanted inventory.

FORCED COLLECTIBLE: A collectible that some smart or lucky marketer created. It is an illusion. Examples include those extremely hard-to-get items that become scarce each Christmas time, like famous dolls and little stuffed toys. The supply somehow dries up and the media blows it out of proportion and the price and demand skyrocket, then the subsequent issues and models all benefit in the craze with inflated prices.

FREECYCLE: Giving away for free usable items to others. It's a great way to conserve, and to give.

FREESTYLE PICKING: To drive by a property with a whole bunch of junk pouring out of buildings and approach without an appointment to see if they want to sell some junk; that is, "cold calling." Some of the popular television programs try this technique.

HIGH GRADING: To get in and get all of the best stuff before anyone else does. This happens at estate sales by the family and others before the public sees it. High grading is also going through your pile of finds, selecting the best to purchase, and putting back the things you have second thoughts about.

JUNKIE: A collector or picker who has to buy something every day or go crazy. He needs to feed his passion. He will usually start shaking somewhat as he buys something fantastic.

JUNKIN': The activity of traveling around to various sites, sales and other likely spots looking for treasures in junk and trash and secondhand stuff. See also yard sailing.

JUNQUE OR JUNK: I suppose junque is deluxe or fancy-style junk. I also suppose that junque has been rescued and displayed, where junk is found as is and might not even be disposed of yet. Junk can still be good working items. Don't confuse it with garbage, which can be wet, stinky, and worthless. Trash, on the other hand, is anything that's been thrown away.

KEYSTONE: A term that started in the jewelry trade and means one half of retail or list price. This is what dealers consider a minimum profit margin or 100 percent markup. If you wholesale to dealers, be aware that they will need to at least double their cost before they put it out on the floor. Don't have a heart attack when you return to the store and see this higher price. (After all, you probably sold it to them and got five or ten times your cost.)

LIQUIDATOR: Someone who is in the business of buying and selling slow-moving merchandise. Some entrepreneurs find several interested buyers who will take everything they can turn up. They then contact likely distributors, dealers, and stores finding distressed merchandise at extremely marked down costs. This is profitable to a few creative people.

LOW-BALLING OR LOW-BALL BID: Bidding quite a bit lower than the value of the item, and probably much lower than you would normally bid yourself. You could also do this type of bidding on many more selections, which increases your chance of winning and getting more items at far better prices, which increases profits. Low-ball the bid even if you might not make a deal. Sometimes if you bid too high, they will suspect an even higher value than it's worth. If you can bid and leave the deal open, this is even better. This way you still have a chance to buy it, especially if you really want it. When you find certain stores, dealers or shows that have silent bids, you might try low-balling occasionally.

MERCENARY: Those only in it for the money. This is great if you make a living at picking because you are constantly turning your inventory. Collectors can't understand how the mercenary can give up so many classic pieces; mercenaries can't understand keeping the stuff if there is a buck to be made.

PAPER: Also, ephemera. The documentation, catalogs, letters, books, booklets, advertisements, dealer information, manuals, literature, service information, labels, magazines, journals, diaries, photographs, posters, cards, specifications, price guides, histories, descriptions, copies, autographs, manuscripts, reprints, correspondence, and other paper items about or found with old products. This stuff is collectible and valuable, and also wonderful reference material as you study and research your special topics and fields of interest. Paper with particular value, for example, if you had an item that included a receipt with Frank Sinatra's name, address, and signature, would be called provenance, and may be an item usually worthless, but now incredibly valuable.

PARLAYING: When you start with a dollar and buy something worth more, then sell it up and up with more items, doubling your original investment. There are now television reality shows showing how dealers do just that. You also get the benefit of learning more about collectibles and antiques as you handle more pieces and can relate with more prices. You can parlay a dollar, doubling it just twenty times and end up with a million dollars. If you start out with a thousand, it only takes ten steps. In one day, you can easily parlay your money and finds a couple of times. It's fun to do, but doesn't work if you make bad purchase decisions, don't know how to sell, or if you want to keep everything you buy.

PICKER: A professional merchant, scrounger, collector, finder, or forager specializing in one or more fields. A picker can be an expert in the values and market of old, useful, and valuable items. One who is constantly looking for antiques and other collectibles or even industrial products. Some of these items can be extremely valuable or historically important in what many people consider junk. The picker finds items for himself or to resell for a profit to dealers and to collectors. A true harvester of good items of value.

PRE-CHASING: An opportunity to preview items included in auctions and finding a customer for those items before they are even your property.

When you bid on the items, you already know for sure how much your customer will pay and how many they will buy from you. An awful lot of smart profit is made every day this way. There are folks who make a comfortable living doing just this. Some crafty businessmen never even touch the product. They bid, buy, and then they ship it off to their customer and keep the profit. You need to realize, however, that there could be many other bidders in attendance at the auction who are doing the same thing. They might have even contacted the same potential customer you did.

PRE-ESTATE SALE: A sell-off of an estate or collection before the public has a chance to know about it. You might just luck upon it or hear about it by word of mouth. Sometimes you are contacted because of advertising you do or your reputation in a certain market. You might get a call like, "You need to call Mrs. Doe. She said her basement is full of her husband's collection which she wants to get rid of." If it had gone on an estate sale, you'd probably never have a chance. If you are fortunate, you might view the collection, make a deal, pay for, and pack away the entire lot. You might have the opportunity to select and purchase just the best pieces (see high-grading). You usually have a wonderful time sorting through all of the stuff at your own pace because there is no competition fighting you for the best stuff. In fact, your competition will probably never hear about it, unless you tell them.

PRE-SELECTING: When you are given a chance to purchase items before an auction is held or before a public advertised sale. This happens rarely, and is usually for family, friends, or employees, but sometimes special customers who have a good buying record are invited to do pre-selecting. When items are auctioned from government agencies, they often allow pre-selecting to adjoining agencies.

PROVENANCE: An antique that comes with the original paperwork, and receipt and other proof of its history. The paperwork might have an autograph of someone famous. It could have special markings, and these markings are visible in history books or journals. The provenance can add a substantial value to your item.

RECYCLE: Trash to be recycled, usually ground melted or processed into similar product, like cardboard, plastic, or glass.

RE-DO: I sold an old cool chrome microphone to an artist recently. He said he was going to use it in a sculpture of a robot he was making. "It will make a fine robot head," he said.

REPURPOSE: Old items made into crafts, furniture, or art. You can easily see what it used to be.

RESCUE: The act of finding vintage and classic collectors' items before they find a way to the landfill.

RE-USE: For example, clothing re-cut and sewn, or glass bottles now used as a lamp, etc.

SALTED AUCTION: Where the auction firm will bring in a load of items from many different sources, even many commercially available products. For example, if you go to an "estate sale" and find twenty oriental rugs or a gun collection being sold by a third party. The extra items are out of place, but convenient for the auction company to sell a bit extra.

SALVAGE: Finding value in garbage or excess product. Salvage yards are gold mines.

SALVAGER OR SCRAPPER: A recycler. Many times, when processing junk and products, some refuse has some scrap or salvage value. Metals and even precious metals can be obtained and bring extra profits. Sometimes just piling it up and occasionally turning it in for cash can be worthwhile. Salvaging not only pertains to metals, but also can include any material that has residual value that can be recycled.

SCRAP: The interesting part of this word could be "crap." But that could turn into dollars! I have found gold in scrap electronics for example. See my Kindle eBook: *E-Waste Gold*

SCALPER: Knows his product and what his customer wants and needs. He asks and gets top dollar. He is a mercenary.

SCOUTS: Used booksellers have been naming their pickers scouts. Book scouts are a valuable resource for book dealers to fulfill their constant need for inventory. Many book scouts are university students trying to augment their income. The book market is divided into countless specialties, which require study and experience. Knowledgeable book scouts can do extremely well. Scouts work the same places as antiques and collectibles pickers—estate sales, thrift stores, etc.

SCROUNGER, SCAVENGER, AND RUMMAGER: Describe picking at the lower end of the scale. These could be aimless pack rats that buy stuff just because. But realize this: they are still your competition. They will buy items before you get a chance and might get in your way.

SMALLS: Many times you will see in antiques stores a glass case with tiny antiques and collectibles. These are sometimes overlooked items that sometimes have a very good value and profit margin. Look for these smalls when you are out and about. It might be a little toy, an advertising specialty, or just an old knickknack.

STEAMPUNK: A new phenomenon where interesting artwork and attire is made from old materials mixed with new tech, to make into old-fashioned trendy items. It gives pickers a whole new market for junk they find. You can then advertise your stuff online, or at shows, etc. as "steampunk" and people will buy it.

SURPLUS: A "key" word for pickers. Excess products are available for pennies on the dollar. Look in phone books, and online for your local city name, etc. You will find surplus stores with mountains of inventory for you.

UPCYCLE: A great "new" word for cool recycling. For example, making clipboards from old electronic circuit boards, purses from license plates, etc. Just put the word "upcycle" in Pinterest and see many more examples.

VINTAGE: This has to do with the age of the item. Vintage, relating to fine aged wine, has given an interesting accent to all kinds of collectibles. So now, vintage clothing, vintage toys, vintage cars, etc. mean more than just old stuff. It's something made long ago from a certain period that is now collectible and valuable.

YARD SAILING: Usually lots of fun, but often not too productive. When you get up early and go out randomly hitting yard sales and garage sales, and maybe even luck upon an estate sale, you are yard sailing. This is all chance and luck. You could be surprised and find a real treasure or waste lots of time and gas. An improved method is to "chart a course" based on what interesting ads you see in the classifieds in the paper or online. If you also focus on areas of the city that typically are old and established, you'll do better. The planned map always beats luck and chance. You can still stop randomly at certain sales you see along the way. You have to get out early, as it's all over by noon. I think if someone could get it started, they might have success with ads that say, "Late afternoon yard sale, come here after you're through with the early sales."

Resources

Here are some websites that can be helpful to pickers, as well as collectors and dealers:

www.pickersbible.com: Author's website, where picking tips and stories are shared.

krausebooks.com: Has a variety of antiques and collectibles books, including industry staples *Antique Trader Antiques and Collectibles Price Guide* and *Warman's Antiques & Collectibles Price Guide*, and books on coins, jewelry, glassware, pottery, toys, and other subjects.

Antique Trader magazine & www. antiquetrader.com: *Antique Trader* has served the antiques and collectibles community since 1957. It is a top resource in antiques and collectibles, offering antiques event calendars, expert columnists, art and antiques auction prices, appraisal values, antiques collecting news and free weekly newsletters at antiquetrader. com.

www.brimfield.com: Site of the largest outdoor antiques show in New England, with over 5,000 dealers from across the country. Includes complete list of show dates, maps, list of dealers, tips, etc.

www.instappraisal.com: A community of more than 100,000 collectors and appraisers from all over the world, who share insight, knowledge, and adventures.

Pickershotline.com: Connects sellers of antiques with pickers looking to buy, and auctions with auctioneers.

www.storagetreasures.com: The internet's leading storage auction information portal, online storage auction marketplace, and local self storage locator. The site also serves auctioneers, appraisers, pickers, yard sale buyers, self storage customers, and facility owners throughout the US and Canada.

estatesales.org: A comprehensive resource for finding estate sales in your local area, and also provides tools for estate liquidators to market their sales online.

www.auctionbloopers.com: This site helps you take advance of eBay seller's misspellings and typos, which can give you a better chance at winning an auction.

fleaportal.com: The gateway to the world of flea markets and provides useful information on flea markets across the country including location, days and hours of operation, number of vendors, contact information, etc.

www.auctiondirectory.us: A directory of all auctions including online auctions, auction houses, and auctioneers.

Index

∙∙∙∙∙∙∙∙∙∙∙∙∙∙∙∙∙∙∙∙∙∙∙∙∙∙∙∙

TOP COLLECTOR GUIDES
FOR ANY HOBBYIST

KrauseBooks.com is your one-stop shop for all of your hobby and collecting needs. Whether you are just getting started or have been collecting for years, our products will help you build, identify, appraise and maintain your collections.

You'll find great products at great prices throughout the site and we even offer **FREE Shipping** on purchases over $49.

Be sure to sign up for to receive exclusive offers and discounts!

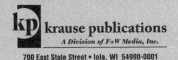